HARLEY-DAVIDSON
BUYER'S GUIDE 1984-2011

PETER GANTRIIS
AND DAIN GINGERELLI

motorbooks

First published in 2011 by MBI Publishing Company LLC and Motorbooks, an imprint of MBI Publishing Company, 400 First Avenue North, Suite 300, Minneapolis, MN, 55401 USA

MBI Publishing Company titles are also available at discounts in bulk quantity for industrial or sales-promotional use. For details write to Special Sales Manager at MBI Publishing Company, 400 First Avenue North, Suite 300, Minneapolis, MN, 55401 USA

Library of Congress Cataloging-in-Publication data

Gantriis, Peter, 1970–
 Harley-Davidson buyer's guide : 1984–2010 / Peter Gantriis; photographs, Greg Field and Doug Mitchel.
   p. cm.
 Includes index.
 ISBN 978-0-7603-3859-9 (pbk. : alk. paper)
 1. Harley-Davidson motorcycle—History. 2. Harley-Davidson motorcycle—Purchasing. I. Title.
 TL448.H3G36 2011
 629.227′5—dc22
                                        2010024313

Editors: Jeffrey Zuehlke and Darwin Holmstrom
Design Manager: Kou Lor
Layout by: Mandy Kimlinger

Printed in China

On the frontis: *Photo by Doug Mitchel*

On the title page: *Photo by Greg Field*

On the cover, main: *Photo by Greg Field*

Dain Gingerelli

Dain Gingerelli has been a motorcycle enthusiast since 1965, and he began writing for motorcycle and automotive magazines in 1970. He's been an editor for six motorcycle titles, and he's authored numerous hot rod books for Motorbooks. Prior to *365 Motorcycles You Must Ride*, he completed his first motorcycle book, *Harley-Davidson Museum Masterpieces*, with photographer Randy Leffingwell. Dain lives in Mission Viejo, California, with his wife and two sons.

Peter Gantriis

Peter Gantriis is founder and president of RPM Research LLC, a market research and consulting firm that works with the world's leading automotive and powersports manufacturers. Peter specializes in market analysis and product development consulting with powersport OEMs. Peter is an avid motorcycle and powersports enthusiast, and he lives in St. Paul with his wife and two sons.

Contents

Introduction

Buying a used Harley-Davidson motorcycle has never been easier—and tougher—to do. It's easier because today's used-bike market is flooded with pre-owned Harleys, so there's plenty of bikes to choose from. Buying a used Harley is tougher to do because there have been so many *models* of Harley-Davidsons made that selecting the right one requires a little research on your part.

Let's get the tough part out of the way first. The 2006 model lineup (which was the last year of the Twin Cam 88 line and pretty much the terminus for this book) boasted 34 variations of models (excluding the four CVO models that compose H-D's special-build division) that were based on five platforms (Sportster, Dyna, Softail, Touring, and V-Rod). Twenty years before that the 1986

model range numbered a baker's dozen, only one more than the 12 available for 1966. In the past 20 years, Harley-Davidson has more than tripled the number of models to choose from.

Muddying the waters even more is what some people term the Harley alphabet. You know the drill: There's the 1948 UL, the 1957 FLHF, the 1984 FXRT, the 1990 FLSTC, the 2001 FXSTI, and most recently the tongue-twisting 2009 FLHTCUTG. The first two letters in a model's designation denote the platform on which the bike is based, followed by the alphabet soup describing the bike's primary features.

Armed with this knowledge (and the necessary cash!) anybody can set out to buy a used Harley-Davidson motorcycle. And that's

where this book comes into play. It offers helpful tips on what to look for and how to go about doing it.

Is *The Harley-Davidson Buyer's Guide* the absolute source to use when shopping for a used Hog? Absolutely not. But it can help you shake out some of the models that you *don't* want to consider, and conversely assist you in deciding which of America's favorite V-twin-powered motorcycles are best suited for you. In the course of that research you can learn about the models' shortcomings and strong points to assist you further in your research. The last thing you want to do is waste your time and your money.

Which brings us to another key point: This book is not a price guide. Like most free-market commodities, used-bike prices fluctuate. Never has it been so evident on the Harley-Davidson front than the past few years when America's economy plunged into the worst economic recession since the Great Depression. Given that, if you can't afford to lose money on a motorcycle, then don't buy a Harley-Davidson as an investment. Instead, you should treat it for what it was intended to be in the first place—a motorcycle that can be ridden, giving you the most enjoyment possible for your dollar. As a biker, you know that there's no greater joy than to be on the open road aboard your favorite motorcycle.

And that brings up the final question when shopping for a used Hog: What's the best Harley-Davidson for you? The answer is as simple as the question. The bike that you're most happy with!

Chapter 1
How to Buy a Used Harley-Davidson

When it comes to purchasing a used motorcycle, the smart money is on a Harley-Davidson. There are two reasons for this. First, history shows us that Harleys retain their value as well as any other brand on the market today. Whether you're considering a current-model Twin Cam or a vintage flathead, Harleys are sound investments in terms of value per dollar and in recouping your money when it's time to sell. Second—and foremost among Harley enthusiasts—this American-made brand rewards owners with miles and miles of riding pleasure. For more than 100 years Harley riders have enjoyed taking to the open road aboard their motorcycles. That great American riding ritual shows no sign of diminishing, which means there should always be enthusiasts willing to purchase used Harleys.

If you haven't done so already, then perhaps it's time to climb aboard and join the fun; it's time for you to buy a used Harley-Davidson motorcycle.

That leads to the next question: Which Harley model should you consider? We've already established in this book's introduction that the best Harley for you is the one that you like. Having said that, do you want a vintage Harley, a bike that is rudimentary by today's standards but boasts old-school character that you can't find in any of today's modern motorcycles? And if you favor an older bike, are you buying it for an investment or as a rider? Will it be a bike that you won't hesitate to take onto the highway? Or do you want a newer model Harley that possesses all the features and amenities that modern motorcycle technology has to offer, making it a bike that you can ride anywhere anytime?

Chances are that if you're shopping for a classic or vintage Harley, you're already familiar with certain models. If you've done your homework, you know as much as you should about the prospective vintage Harleys that you seek. If you're not as knowledgeable about these older bikes as you feel you should be for a purchase, it might be wise to find an expert who you can rely on for valuable insight and feedback. Doing so could save you money in the long run. With that in mind, let's confine this discussion to current model years, which is to say 1984 and up.

The post-1983 era represents the "new" Harley-Davidson Motor Company. These are the years in which bikes were conceived and developed by members of the consortium that bought the company in 1981 from American Machine and Foundry (AMF). While there have been plenty of different models offered since 1984, practically all have been based on one of five basic platforms: Sportster (XL), Dyna (FX and its predecessor, the FXR), Softail (FX or FLS), Touring (FL), and V-Rod (VRSC).

It was in 1984 that the Big Twin engine received its first major redesign since the overhead-valve E-model originally bowed in 1936. The all-new 1984 Evolution V2 engine (a.k.a., Evo) elevated Harley-Davidson to a higher level in the general motorcycle market. The 80-cubic-inch alloy engine produced more power and dripped less oil than the Shovelhead model that it replaced, and for the most part Evo owners were rewarded with bikes that were as reliable as any Harley-Davidson model ever before.

But be warned: Some bikes from 1984, and even 1985, were built using parts and components that were carryovers from the Shovelhead era. In an effort to maximize profit margins for various new models, production managers scrounged leftover parts to adapt to newer models. Some mechanics call these bikes "parts bin specials." Be wary of bikes from these years because pinpointing the exact replacement part numbers can be tricky.

By 1986 some of the technology found in the Evo was incorporated into the Sportster motor. The new Sportster engine was available as 883-cc or 1,000-cc models. More change came in 1999 when Harley introduced yet another design—the Twin Cam 88—to replace the aging 80-inch Evo motor that had been on the market since 1984.

Despite these and many other engineering improvements, the heart and soul of Harley's V-twin design (Big Twins and Sportsters) remained unchanged. You might say that the Motor Company has been on a roll, offering enthusiasts modern-day classic motorcycles that mix the pleasures of everyday riding with the nostalgic charm and heritage associated with yesteryear motorcycling.

So it's the models with Evo and Twin Cam engines that you'll more than likely be shopping for, because these are the Harleys that practically beg to be ridden, making them popular among enthusiasts. The general specifications and basic descriptions of these models are included elsewhere in this book, so use them to become familiar with the various models. Armed with that information, the actual process of shopping for bikes and examining them to see whether or not they're worth buying becomes a matter of "dos" and "don'ts" associated with buying any used motorcycle. So let's talk about some of the major dos and don'ts of used Harley shopping.

Before continuing, there's a minor caveat to consider: Some authorized Harley-Davidson dealers prefer *not* to work on motorcycles 10 or more years old. That means absolutely no Harleys with Evolution engines in their service shop—Twin Cams, late-model Sportsters, and V-Rods only, please. So if you have a used Evo model in your sights, you might check to see if there's a reputable independent shop near you that takes in pre-Twin Cam models for service. You'd be surprised at the number of shops that specialize in older Harleys like this.

When the time comes to single out a bike for a closer look, a major point to consider is the amount of add-ons that might be on the bike itself. It's a fact: Harley-Davidson owners like to personalize their bikes, so the chance of finding an absolutely original or stock-condition Harley is slim to none. Aftermarket exhausts, seats, handlebars, hand grips, control levers and pedals, passenger or sissy bars, wheels and tires, even custom paint jobs, are commonly found on used Harleys. Depending on what items the owner selected to personalize his or her bike, you'll face a decision: Do these add-ons suit your tastes in terms of style and riding comfort? If not, you might want to walk away at that point—unless the bike itself is in extraordinary condition, making it too good to pass up. That's when you can dig a little deeper into the bike's history. Does the owner still have all the original parts that were removed that he can include in the deal? If not, how much money and time would it require to chase

down the replacement components to restore the bike to a condition more suitable to your tastes?

You should also consider the bike's wheels. Harleys come with either cast-aluminum or laced-spoke wheels and rims. Cast wheels have a clear advantage; they make it possible for quick roadside flat-tire repairs because they have no inner tube. Although laced-spoke rims give a bike a more nostalgic appearance, those spokes also mean there's an inner tube, so you can't use a quick-patch on them should you get a flat tire. They're also more time consuming to clean compared to cast or polished forged wheels.

Check for crash damage too. Telltale signs of a mishap often show up on the ends of the handgrips and levers. Dents or scratches in the gas tank or fenders can be further evidence of a lay down. Chassis damage such as a bent frame or fork legs can be tougher to spot, but sometimes you can see that a frame has been damaged by checking the final-drive belt or the chain's alignment. Another way to examine for bent chassis components is to look for unusual wear patterns in the tire tread. If the fork doesn't line up with the frame, the front and rear tires probably won't be in alignment. It's as simple as that.

You can also conduct a quick inspection of the engine, transmission, and primary drive first by checking for oil leaks. If they pass muster, ask the owner to fire up the engine and then listen for strange noises while the engine idles. If the owner won't allow a test ride, then ask to put the transmission into gear and give the clutch lever a gentle release to feel for drag or slip (and more strange noises). After the engine is shut off, check for oil leaks again just to make sure.

These are just a few quick tips to help you get started in your search for a used Harley. Perhaps the best advice is to be patient and take your time when examining a bike. Try to view it in the daylight so you can see all the detail. Finally, if the bike looks really good, investing a few more dollars for a qualified mechanic to give it a closer look might be worth the money. After all, you're talking about a bike that also happens to be an investment on your part.

About the ratings:
The star system works as follows:
★ Not collectible, impractical
★★ Marginally collectible, marginally practical
★★★ Average collectibility, average practicality
★★★★ Very collectible, very useable
★★★★★ The most collectible, the most useable

The year 1984 was a pivotal one in the history of the Harley-Davidson Motor Company, and the FXR is a pivotal model in Harley-Davidson history. Amidst the drama of the tariff hearings (Harley CEO Vaughn Beals' appeal to the U.S. government for protection against the Big Four Japanese—a story for another book), Harley was under pressure to launch new and improved products. The buyout from AMF occurred in June 1981 and left the Motor Company with an enormous debt. To say money was tight would be an understatement. During the summer of 1982, the newly formed company was in violation of its creditor terms and in a real risk of foreclosure.

Development of the new Evolution engine had actually started in 1976, while AMF was still the owner of Harley-Davidson. Two energetic engineers, Vaughn Beals and Jeffrey Bleustein, made the case to develop a replacement to the venerable Shovelhead. The Shovelhead design was never going to be able to meet the increasingly stringent emissions regulations and durability requirements of a rapidly changing marketplace, and they knew it. Beals and Bleustein proposed to develop two completely new powertrains: an improved air-cooled V-twin and a liquid-cooled engine.

Development of the liquid-cooled engine was ultimately outsourced to Porsche, but the air-cooled mill remained in-house. The result was the Evolution, an engine that would go on to transform not only the motorcycles it powered but the Harley-Davidson Motor Company itself.

The first bikes to receive the Evo engine were the FLTC, FLHTC, FXRS, FXST, and FXRT. Harley hedged its commitment to the Evo by maintaining production of the Shovelhead engine and offering it in the FLH and FX chassis. There were two key reasons why Harley wanted to continue production of the Shovelhead. First, there was some trepidation about the Evo's reliability and performance. Second, there remained a real fear of alienating the die-hard Harley traditionalists who would not want to trade up to a new Evo-powered bike.

Sales of Evo-powered bikes accelerated through 1983–84. The FXR chassis was introduced with the 1981 FXR Superglide, and it served as an excellent platform in which to mount the Evo engine.

This FXR chassis was narrow, stylish, and the torsion was rigid. As a result, the FXRT had plenty of boulevard attention-grabbing style, yet it was also capable as both a sporting mount and a lightweight touring bike. With its narrow profile and ample ground clearance, the FXRT was able to carve the turns and fulfill its mission as a performance bike. This unique blend of improved performance, style, and touring capability make the FXRT a milestone bike in Harley history.

As it turned out, the Evo was well-received at its introduction. Upon testing the initial Evo-powered bikes, the motorcycling press took a favorable view. *Cycle Magazine* noted that its Evo test bike (a 1984 FXRT) outperformed the Shovelhead in almost every category. Horsepower and torque were improved, and the drivability was far better than the Shovel. Harley's big gamble on the Evo was paying off.

1984 FXR 1340 Sport Glide specifications

Drivetrain

Engine:	Evolution
Layout:	45-degree V-twin
Displacement:	82 cubic inches (1,337 cc)
Cooling:	Air-cooled
Compression ratio:	8.5:1
Fuel system:	Carbureted
Horsepower:	64.0 @ 5,200 rpm
Primary drive:	Chain, 34/46 ratio
Transmission:	Five-speed
Final drive:	Belt

Chassis

Fuel capacity:	5.0 gallons
Oil capacity:	3.5 quarts
Wheelbase:	64.7 inches
Weight:	658 pounds (wet)
Seat height (unlade):	25.5 inches

Suspension

Front:	Telescopic fork
Rear:	Twin shocks

Brakes

Front:	2 disc
Rear:	1 disc
Wheels:	19 inches (front), 16 inches (rear)

What they said

"...The most competent and truly versatile Harley we've ever ridden."
—*Cycle Magazine* (1985 FXRS)

"For those who wanted to see if Harley could build a real, honest-to-Davidson 1984 motorcycle, feast your eyes. The '84 season is here—and Harley is right here with it."—*Motorcyclist* (1984 FXRT)

"V-twins provide a special kind of conveyance. When in a hurry, riding the bleak, straight, boring interstates and knocking back 500 or 600 miles a day, the Gold Wings and Voyagers are certainly the best ways of getting there. But when I'm touring—riding back roads, watching the scenery and using time instead of trying to beat it—the easygoing pace of a big V is more conducive to my mood and purpose. These days I think more and more often about buying a touring bike, and now the FXRT has joined the Yamaha Venture at the top of my list."—*Motorcyclist*, December, 1984 (1985 FXRT)

"We just wanted something that you didn't have to oil or adjust, that didn't spray oil all over you. We got all that, but the belts also lasted much longer and looked better too." —Vaughan Beals (referring to the belt final drive, 1985 Big Twin models)

Parts prices/cost of typical repairs

Parts and Ownership Costs: Typical H-D dealer labor rate = $90/hour

Maintenance item	Action	Interval*	Estimated cost
Air filter	Inspect, service as required		$12.95
Air suspension	Check pressure, operation, and leakage	Annually	
Base gasket	Inspect as necessary		7.5 hours labor $750 total @ dealer
Battery	Check battery and clean connections. Old flooded-type batteries should be immediately replaced.	Annually	
Brake fluid	Check levels and condition	Check level annually. Flush and replace with new fluid every 2 years	
Brake pads and discs	Inspect for wear	Replace as needed	
Clutch	Check adjustment		
Critical fasteners	Check tightness	Every 5,000 miles	
Cruise control	Inspect disengage switch and components	As required	
Drive belt and sprockets	Inspect, adjust belt	Adjustment should be performed by dealer	
Electrical equipment and switches	Check operation		
Engine oil and filter	Replace	Every 5,000 miles	
Fork oil	Replace	Every 10,000 miles	2.5 hours labor $275 total @ dealer
Fuel door and saddlebags	Lubricate hinges and latches	As required	
Fuel lines and fittings	Inspect for leaks	Annually	
Jiffy stand	Inspect and lubricate	Annually	
Oil lines and system	Inspect for leaks	Annually	
Primary chain case lubricant	Replace	Every 10,000 miles	
Spark plugs	Inspect	Replace every 20,000 miles	
Steering head bearings	Lubricate	50,000 miles	
Throttle, brake, clutch controls	Check, adjust, and lubricate		
Tires	Check pressure, inspect tread		
Transmission lubricant	Replace	Every 20,000 miles	
Wheel spokes	Check tightness		
Wheel bearings			.6 hours labor $120 total @ dealer
Three-fluid change	(Crankcase, primary, transmission oils)		.3 hours labor $170 total @ dealer
20,000 mile service	3 fluid change, all req. maint Check spark plugs		$700 total @ dealer

Note: If the bike has been unused and in storage for more than three years, all of these items should receive immediate attention, and key fluids and lubricants should be drained and replaced.

Usability and collectibility ratings

Usability: ★★★★ Except for a pillowy stock seat that appeared comfortable on the showroom, but was a torture device in the real world, this is one of the most practical all-around motorcycles that Harley-Davidson ever produced.

Collectibility: ★ Though this bike is rare, it is rare because it was unpopular and also because those few bikes Harley did sell often became donors for custom projects.

Garage Watch
Key items to look for.

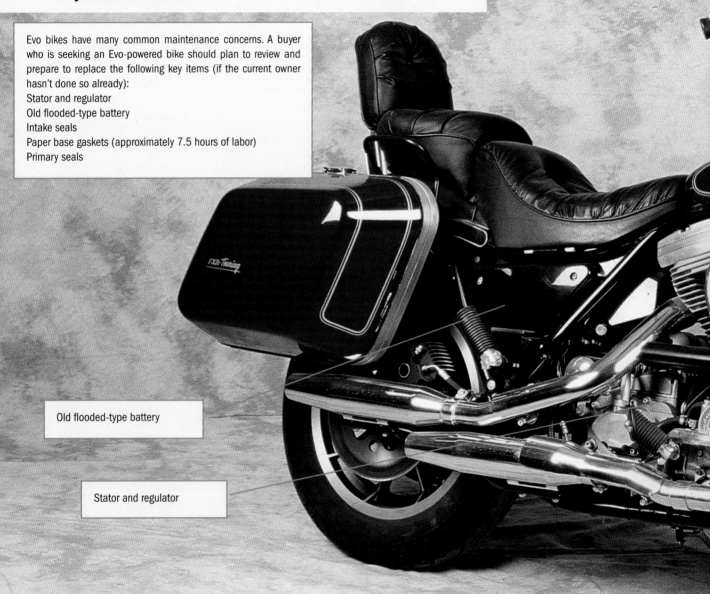

Evo bikes have many common maintenance concerns. A buyer who is seeking an Evo-powered bike should plan to review and prepare to replace the following key items (if the current owner hasn't done so already):
Stator and regulator
Old flooded-type battery
Intake seals
Paper base gaskets (approximately 7.5 hours of labor)
Primary seals

Old flooded-type battery

Stator and regulator

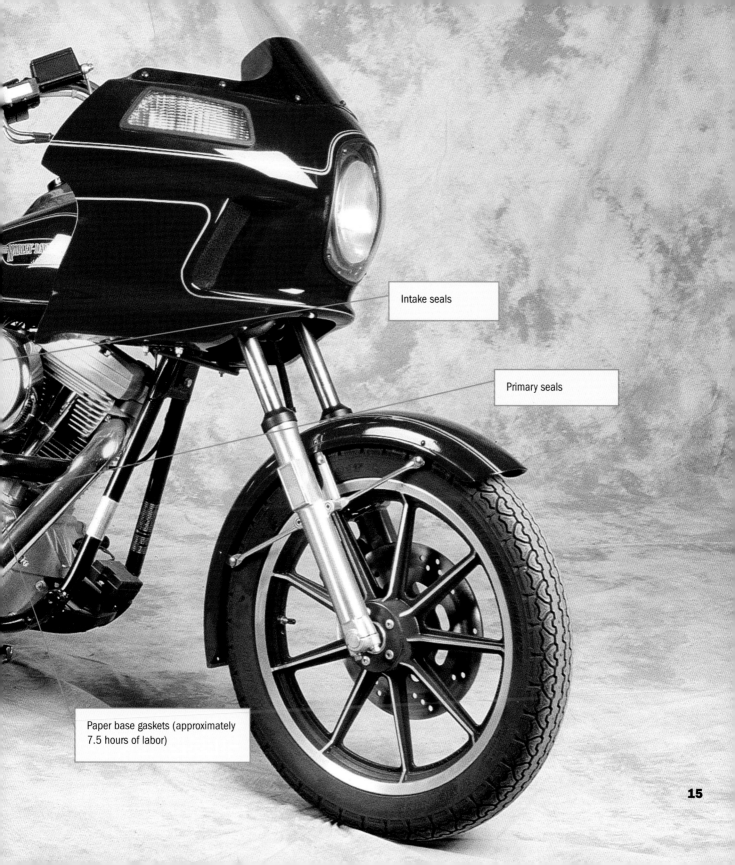

Intake seals

Primary seals

Paper base gaskets (approximately 7.5 hours of labor)

Chapter 3
1984 to 1998 FLHTCU

In the early 1980s, Harley had two main Touring bike models, the FLT and FLH. The FLHT was released in spring 1983 as a blend of the roadworthy FLT Tour Glide and the stylish FLH. The base for the new FLHT was the rubber-mounted chassis of the FLT. Harley engineers integrated the handlebar-mounted "bat wing" fairing and successfully achieved the classic style that buyers wanted in the new model. Now dubbed the Electra Glide, the bike quickly became a mainstay of the Harley Touring family.

Over the ensuing years, the Electra Glide received a steady stream of updates and improvements. The Evo-powered Electra Glides arrived in 1984. In addition, the '84 bikes received substantial chassis improvements. An adjustable air-suspension system was fitted at each end of the bike, and the front suspension used the anti-dive technology that was introduced in the FXRT. A revised braking system included larger discs for the front brakes and new calipers. In 1985, the Electra Glide received a belt final drive, substantially reducing driveline maintenance. In 1986, the cockpit received substantial changes. The inner fairings and handlebar controls were redesigned to integrate the gauge package and the now-standard AM/FM/cassette/CB system.

A couple of limited-edition models were offered in 1985. About 600 FLHTC were colored with a unique two-tone maroon paint scheme. There were also 800 Liberty Edition bikes that were sold as a tribute to the restoration of the Statue of Liberty. These bikes were painted Blackberry and silver, with special "Ride Free" graphics. Harley-Davidson donated $100 from the sale of each of these bikes to the statue's restoration fund. These two limited-edition bikes should be considered among the most collectible Harley Touring bikes of this era.

The pace of development accelerated into the late 1980s and early 1990s. Honda had introduced its six-cylinder Gold Wing in 1988, and the luxurious bike sent shockwaves across the motorcycle marketplace. To keep pace, Harley added many more luxury and convenience features to the Electra Glide and dubbed the new 1989 model the Ultra Classic.

The Ultra is a mix of Harley style and modern amenities. The 1989 Ultra was loaded with every amenity that Harley had in the catalog, plus some new ones. The functional improvements included new fairing lowers (with locking glove compartments) and wind deflectors, electronic cruise control, and additional lighting on the TourPak. A powerful digitally tuned stereo provided background music for the long rides, and the intercom system greatly aided communication with the passenger. To set it apart from its stable mates, the Ultra received special two-tone paint and a black-and-chrome engine. There were penalties, however, for the long list of amenities. To keep the electronics functioning, Harley had to install the 32-amp alternator from the police bikes, and the bike's curb weight ballooned to nearly 800 pounds. Nevertheless, the Ultra sold very well, and by the end of the 1980s, the Electra Glide models were outselling the Tour Glide models by a 4-to-1 margin.

1984 FLHTCU specifications

Drivetrain

Engine:	Evolution
Layout:	45-degree V-twin
Displacement:	82 cubic inches (1,337 cc)
Cooling:	Air-cooled
Compression ratio:	8.5:1
Fuel system:	Carburetor
Horsepower:	64.0 @ 5,200 rpm
Primary drive:	Chain
Transmission:	Five-speed
Final drive:	Enclosed chain

Chassis

Fuel capacity:	5.0 gallon
Wheelbase:	64.7 inches
Weight:	658 pounds (wet)
Seat height (unlade):	25.5 inches

Suspension

Front:	Telescopic fork
Rear:	Twin air adjustable shocks

Brakes

Front:	2 disc
Rear:	1 disc
Wheels:	16 inches (front), 16 inches (rear)

What they said

"One important element that separates Harley's touring bikes from the rest of the company's line is the use of air-assisted suspension on the dressers. It's a good idea, but poorly executed. Pressure is adjusted via a Schrader valve awkwardly placed between the left passenger footrest and the left saddlebag. Since air pressure must be checked with the machine on its side-stand–it has to be centerstand–you really have to reach down to access the valve. And the air system has so little overall capacity that to merely check the pressure is to reduce it by at least a little. Likewise, just a touch with a typical gas-station hose–there is no onboard compressor-rockets the pressure into the stratosphere."–*Cycle World*, November 1992 (1993 FLHT)

"I packed the Ultra, left Los Angeles at five Friday morning, rolled into 'Frisco by noon, met Rick at one, got to the show at four, rocked my socks off 'til midnight and left the following morning, hoarse, to be at the Vance & Hines 24-hour victory party in Los Angeles by five that night. The trip was hectic and I was dragging by the end, but the Harley chugged along without complaint, spewing vintage Springsteen into my helmet and pampering my bottom all the way. Roding to see an all-American rock'n'roller on an all-American motorcycle–like the American beer commercial says, 'It doesn't get much better than this.'"– *Motorcyclist*, December 1988

Parts prices/cost of typical repairs

Parts and Ownership Costs: Typical H-D dealer labor rate = $90/hour

Maintenance item	Action	Interval*	Estimated cost
Air filter	Inspect, service as required		$12.95
Air suspension	Check pressure, operation, and leakage	Annually	
Base gasket	Inspect as necessary		7.5 hours labor $750 total @ dealer
Battery	Check battery and clean connections. Old flooded-type batteries should be immediately replaced.	Annually	
Brake fluid	Check levels and condition	Check level annually. Flush and replace with new fluid every 2 years	
Brake pads and discs	Inspect for wear	Replace as needed	
Clutch	Check adjustment		
Critical fasteners	Check tightness	Every 5,000 miles	
Cruise control	Inspect disengage switch and components	As required	
Drive belt and sprockets	Inspect, adjust belt	Adjustment should be performed by dealer	
Electrical equipment and switches	Check operation		
Engine oil and filter	Replace	Every 5,000 miles	
Fork oil	Replace	Every 10,000 miles	2.5 hours labor $275 total @ dealer
Fuel door and saddlebags	Lubricate hinges and latches	As required	
Fuel lines and fittings	Inspect for leaks	Annually	
Jiffy stand	Inspect and lubricate	Annually	
Oil lines and system	Inspect for leaks	Annually	
Primary chain case lubricant	Replace	Every 10,000 miles	
Spark plugs	Inspect	Replace every 20,000 miles	
Steering head bearings	Lubricate	50,000 miles	
Throttle, brake, clutch controls	Check, adjust, and lubricate		
Tires	Check pressure, inspect tread		
Transmission lubricant	Replace	Every 20,000 miles	
Wheel spokes	Check tightness		
Wheel bearings			.6 hours labor $120 total @ dealer
Three-fluid change	(Crankcase, primary, transmission oils)		.3 hours labor $170 total @ dealer
20,000 mile service	3 fluid change, all req. maint Check spark plugs		$700 total @ dealer

Note: If the bike has been unused and in storage for more than three years, all of these items should receive immediate attention, and key fluids and lubricants should be drained and replaced.

Usability and collectibility ratings

Usability: ★★★★ The first generation touring frames had a tendency to flex around their rubber motor mounts, but the rider gets used to this. In the right hands, an Electra Glide can hold its own when the road gets twisty.

Collectibility: ★★★ These were popular and well-loved motorcycles, but there are too many of them on the road for them to ever become blue-chip collectors items.

Recalls and service bulletins

The 1994–98 Ultras were recalled for electrical failure issues. Excessive current could cause a loss of electric power through the ignition switch and cause the bike to stall, run erratically, or fail to start. Dealers replaced ignition switch/circuit breakers and installed a relay kit.

Garage Watch
Key items to look for.

Evo bikes have many common maintenance concerns. A buyer who is seeking an Evo-powered bike should plan to review and prepare to replace the following key items (if the current owner hasn't done so already):
Stator and regulator
Old flooded-type battery
Intake seals
Paper base gaskets (approximately 7.5 hours of labor)
Primary seals

Old flooded-type battery

Final drive belt reliable but difficult and expensive to replace when worn out.

Stator and regulator

Primary seals

Ignition switch should have been replaced under recall (1994–98)

Intake seals

Paper base gaskets (approximately 7.5 hours of labor)

Chapter 4
1984 to 1996 FLT

The V2 Evolution was a huge step forward in engine technology for Harley, and it debuted in the FXR bikes. Shortly thereafter, the Touring bikes became beneficiaries of the new engine's technology and durability.

Harley's flagship touring bike through the 1980s was the FLT Tour Glide. The FLT arrived in the fall of 1979 as a direct competitor to the Honda Gold Wing Interstate (also introduced as a 1980 model), and it received positive reviews from both riders and the motorcycling press. Some unique features set the FLT apart from the competition; key among them is the "balanced fork" steering setup. Hidden beneath the frame-mounted fairing of the FLT is an unorthodox steering head and triple-clamp setup. Developed by Harley engineer Ray Miennert, the FLT's steering head is actually located in front of the fork tubes. This greatly reduces the effort required to steer the 800-pound Touring bike, and it is one of the most revered features of the FLT. Combined with its rubber-mounted chassis, the FLT represented the first significant engineering achievement by Harley since the 1970s, and it cast a positive light on the still-struggling Motor Company.

In 1984, the Evo was fitted in both of the rubber-mounted Touring bikes, the FLT and FLHT. The Evo was a full 20 pounds lighter than the Shovelhead, ran smoother, and was far more oil-efficient. FLT sales spiked that year as buyers clamored for the Evo-powered bikes, but a sales slide soon followed. It is commonly believed that sales were hampered by purists' cool reception to the "shark-nose" styling of the FLT. The controversial style of the FLT was derided as too "Japanese," and buyers quickly migrated toward the more traditionally styled FLHT. Despite the controversy over its styling, the FLT proved that it was a capable long-distance mount. Its capacious top box and saddlebags can accommodate the gear that is required for long journeys, and the comfortable, well-protected saddle is a great place from which to watch the countryside cruise by.

Like the FLHT, the FLT Tour Glide received a steady stream of improvements and additional amenity features. From day one, the FLT has been a well-equipped touring bike—features like a powerful stereo, full instrumentation, and a luxurious cockpit were standard equipment for bikes in this class, and the FLT was so equipped. In 1988, the Ultra Classic Tour Glide package was introduced. The Ultra offered electronic cruise control, CB radio, front and rear sound systems, a passenger intercom, and new fairing lowers. As the 1990s progressed, the FLT received incremental changes to its engine and electronics packages. Sound systems were improved to better integrate with the CB and intercom systems, and other minor tweaks were made to the engine and transmission. For model year 1996, fuel injection was offered as an option on all Touring bikes, the FLT included.

Diminishing sales caused Harley to discontinue the FLT after the 1996 model year. This would only be temporary, however. In 1998, the Motor Company reintroduced the FLT in the form of the FLTR Road Glide, a modern "custom bagger" with a much more contemporary style.

1986 FLTC specifications

Drivetrain
Engine:	Evolution
Layout:	45-degree V-twin
Displacement:	82 cubic inches (1,337 cc)
Cooling:	Air-cooled
Compression ratio:	8.5:1
Fuel system:	Carburetor
Horsepower:	65.0 @ 5,000 rpm
Primary drive:	Chain
Transmission:	Five-speed
Final drive:	Belt

Chassis
Fuel capacity:	4.8 gallons
Wheelbase:	62.9 inches
Weight:	788 pounds (wet)
Seat height (unlade):	31.3 inches

Suspension
Front:	Telescopic fork
Rear:	Twin shocks

Brakes
Front:	2 disc
Rear:	1 disc
Wheels:	16 inches (front), 16 inches (rear)

What they said

"The FLT and FLHT taught us that Harley customers want improvements and modernization, but those have to come with the classic look. That is a real design challenge, but it's also what makes our motorcycles unique."—Tom Gelb, Harley-Davidson (1981 FLT)

"The giant top box and saddlebags will hold all your gear for weeks on the road. The Tour Glide came with a set of tools, something Harley left out for nearly 20 years."—Allan Girdler (1984 FLT)

"The Evolution engine makes more power than the old Shovelhead, but neither mill is going to give the FJ1100 any trouble. The new Blockhead, as it has already been named by the Harley faithful, makes about 10 percent more peak torque than the old engine and, more importantly, should outlast it by tens of thousands of miles. The mill is still no high-horsepower unit, but it does possess strong midrange power—enough to make it the second strongest roll-on performer of the big tourers."
—*Motorcyclist*, October, 1984, 1985 FLT

"Touring in the American idiom simply doesn't get any more American than two 40-inch, air-cooled cylinders splayed 45 degrees apart. Even though two of our Japanese entries are assembled in Nebraska and Ohio, there is something inescapably and essentially American about the primal beat of an 80-inch Milwaukee twin reeling in mile after mile of interstate."
—*Motorcyclist*, June 1990

Parts prices/cost of typical repairs

Parts and Ownership Costs: Typical H-D dealer labor rate = $90/hour

Maintenance item	Action	Interval*	Estimated cost
Air filter	Inspect, service as required		$12.95
Air suspension	Check pressure, operation, and leakage	Annually	
Base gasket	Inspect as necessary		7.5 hours labor $750 total @ dealer
Battery	Check battery and clean connections. Old flooded-type batteries should be immediately replaced.	Annually	
Brake fluid	Check levels and condition	Check level annually. Flush and replace with new fluid every 2 years	
Brake pads and discs	Inspect for wear	Replace as needed	
Clutch	Check adjustment		
Critical fasteners	Check tightness	Every 5,000 miles	
Cruise control	Inspect disengage switch and components	As required	
Drive belt and sprockets	Inspect, adjust belt	Adjustment should be performed by dealer	
Electrical equipment and switches	Check operation		
Engine oil and filter	Replace	Every 5,000 miles	
Fork oil	Replace	Every 10,000 miles	2.5 hours labor $275 total @ dealer
Fuel door and saddlebags	Lubricate hinges and latches	As required	
Fuel lines and fittings	Inspect for leaks	Annually	
Jiffy stand	Inspect and lubricate	Annually	
Oil lines and system	Inspect for leaks	Annually	
Primary chain case lubricant	Replace	Every 10,000 miles	
Spark plugs	Inspect	Replace every 20,000 miles	
Steering head bearings	Lubricate	50,000 miles	
Throttle, brake, clutch controls	Check, adjust, and lubricate		
Tires	Check pressure, inspect tread		
Transmission lubricant	Replace	Every 20,000 miles	
Wheel spokes	Check tightness		
Wheel bearings			.6 hours labor $120 total @ dealer
Three-fluid change	(Crankcase, primary, transmission oils)		.3 hours labor $170 total @ dealer
20,000 mile service	3 fluid change, all req. maint Check spark plugs		$700 total @ dealer

Note: If the bike has been unused and in storage for more than three years, all of these items should receive immediate attention, and key fluids and lubricants should be drained and replaced.

Usability and collectibility ratings

Usability: ★★★★ The frame-mounted fairing of the FLT should work better than the handlebar-mounted fairing on the FLH, but in reality they both work about equally as well. It's a matter of taste more than function.

Collectibility: ★★ Harley buyers never took to the frame-mounted fairing in its original touring form, and these bikes languished on showroom floors. They still are not very popular among the Harley faithful.

Recalls and service bulletins

The 1994–98 Ultras were recalled for electrical failure issues. Excessive current could cause a loss of electric power through the ignition switch and cause the bike to stall, run erratically, or fail to start. Dealers replaced ignition switches and circuit breakers and installed a relay kit.

Garage Watch
Key items to look for.

Evo bikes have many common maintenance concerns. A buyer who is seeking an Evo-powered bike should plan to review and prepare to replace the following key items (if the current owner hasn't done so already):
Stator and regulator
Old flooded-type battery
Intake seals
Paper base gaskets (approximately 7.5 hours of labor)
Primary seals

Old flooded-type battery

Stator and regulator

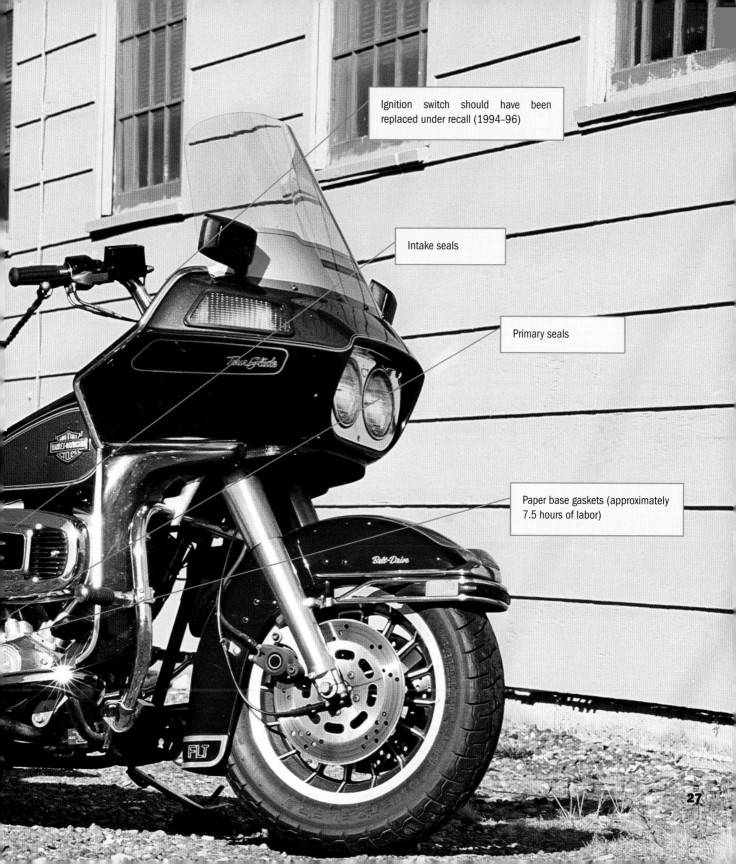

Ignition switch should have been replaced under recall (1994–96)

Intake seals

Primary seals

Paper base gaskets (approximately 7.5 hours of labor)

Chapter 5
1984 to 1985 FXST Softail Standard (Four-speed)

The Softail was introduced in 1984, and it proved to be one of the most important vehicle launch decisions that the Motor Company ever made.

The design history of the Softail is permanently embedded in Harley lore, but we'll share the (very) brief version here. Custom bikes had evolved steadily from the bobbers of the 1950s to the raked-out choppers of the 1960s and 1970s. Custom-bike builders loved the simple "teardrop" profile of rigid, hard-tail frames, and they were typically built on pre-1958 Big Twin frames or on aftermarket. The choppers dispensed with the comfort features found on the FLH, including the sprung seats. Long-haul comfort was far less important than the overall style of the chopper, so sacrifices were necessary.

The growth of the custom bike aftermarket spurred many innovations. Builders recognized that the traditional hardtail style was beautiful, but the bikes' lack of a rear suspension made longer rides a chore. The Softail was born from the design of enthusiast (and mechanical engineer) Bill Davis. While some aftermarket companies pursued a traditional "plunger"-type suspension to smooth out the ride, Davis designed a frame with a unique suspension layout. From the outside, Davis' frame looked like a true hardtail, but under the seat was a triangular swingarm that pivoted. The rear suspension action was damped by twin shocks that were mounted horizontally under the transmission and hidden from view.

The Motor Company was aware of the existence of Davis' design, and in 1982 he sold the design patents to Harley-Davidson. The decision to buy this design was controversial within the Motor Company. Some executives felt that the design was the wrong direction for the company to pursue in the 1980s, but Vaughan Beals, Jeffrey Bleustein, and Willie G. Davidson were emphatically in favor of the new bike.

The result was the introduction of the all-new 1984 FXST Softail. The Softail was built around an all-new chassis that closely reflected Davis' original concept. The designers focused on integrating some key items into the final design, using the successful FXWG as a guide. The long, low, and wide look defines the FXST, and the design used virtually the entire front end of the Wide Glide from the steering head forward. Styling cues like the split fuel tanks, center-mounted speedo, and horseshoe-shaped oil tank recall the classic design elements of the 1936–65 Big Twin bikes. The new Evo engine powered the FXST, but the rest of the driveline was decidedly old school. The Evo engine was hard-mounted to the frame and mated to a four-speed transmission with a kick starter prominently attached.

The FXST was an immediate sales success. Despite some grumbling from the motorcycle press, especially about the lack of rear suspension travel, the Softail was warmly received by both the Harley faithful and the growing group of nontraditional customers. The Softail soared to the top of the Harley sales charts in only its first year. The Softail's combination of custom style and clever engineering yielded an entirely new platform on which to build a family of motorcycles, and this would prove to be important as the Motor Company endured its financial hardships of the early 1980s.

1984 FXST specifications

Drivetrain

Engine:	Evolution
Layout:	45-degree V-twin
Displacement:	82 cubic inches (1,337 cc)
Cooling:	Air-cooled
Compression ratio:	8.5:1
Fuel system:	Carburetor
Horsepower:	65.0 @ 5,000 rpm
Primary drive:	Chain
Transmission:	Four-speed
Final drive:	Chain

Chassis

Engine mount:	Rigid
Fuel capacity:	5.2 gallons
Wheelbase:	66.3 inches
Weight:	52 pounds (wet)
Seat height:	26 inches

Suspension

Front:	Telescopic fork
Rear:	Twin shocks

Brakes

Front:	1 disc
Rear:	1 disc
Wheels:	21 inches (front), 16 inches (rear)

What they said

"Once we had the Softail, we could do all kinds of wondrous things with it." —Vaughan Beals (1984 FXST)

"If you were building a chopper in the '60s or '70s, you might have started with a stock 1950-something Hydra-Glide, extended the fork, fitted a narrow 21-inch front wheel, bobbed the rear fender, and fitted a fender-hugging stepped saddle. And you would have ended up with something that looked pretty much like the 1984 Softail." —*Cycle World*, September, 1993.

Parts prices/cost of typical repairs

Parts and Ownership Costs: Typical H-D dealer labor rate = $90/hour

Maintenance item	Action	Interval*	Estimated cost
Air filter	Inspect, service as required		$12.95
Air suspension	Check pressure, operation, and leakage	Annually	
Base gasket	Inspect as necessary		7.5 hours labor $750 total @ dealer
Battery	Check battery and clean connections. Old flooded-type batteries should be immediately replaced.	Annually	
Brake fluid	Check levels and condition	Check level annually. Flush and replace with new fluid every 2 years	
Brake pads and discs	Inspect for wear	Replace as needed	
Clutch	Check adjustment		
Critical fasteners	Check tightness	Every 5,000 miles	
Cruise control	Inspect disengage switch and components	As required	
Drive belt and sprockets	Inspect, adjust belt	Adjustment should be performed by dealer	
Electrical equipment and switches	Check operation		
Engine oil and filter	Replace	Every 5,000 miles	
Fork oil	Replace	Every 10,000 miles	2.5 hours labor $275 total @ dealer
Fuel door and saddlebags	Lubricate hinges and latches	As required	
Fuel lines and fittings	Inspect for leaks	Annually	
Jiffy stand	Inspect and lubricate	Annually	
Oil lines and system	Inspect for leaks	Annually	
Primary chain case lubricant	Replace	Every 10,000 miles	
Spark plugs	Inspect	Replace every 20,000 miles	
Steering head bearings	Lubricate	50,000 miles	
Throttle, brake, clutch controls	Check, adjust, and lubricate		
Tires	Check pressure, inspect tread		
Transmission lubricant	Replace	Every 20,000 miles	
Wheel spokes	Check tightness		
Wheel bearings			.6 hours labor $120 total @ dealer
Three-fluid change	(Crankcase, primary, transmission oils)		.3 hours labor $170 total @ dealer
20,000 mile service	3 fluid change, all req. maint Check spark plugs		$700 total @ dealer

Note: If the bike has been unused and in storage for more than three years, all of these items should receive immediate attention, and key fluids and lubricants should be drained and replaced.

Usability and collectibility ratings

Usability: ★ With its solid-mounted, unbalanced engine, limited-travel rear suspension, four-speed transmission, and chopper-esque riding position, this one looks better than it rides.

Collectibility: ★★★★★ Though impractical, these were the first factory-built choppers. They were immediately popular and revolutionized the motorcycle industry.

Garage Watch
Key items to look for.

Evo bikes have many common maintenance concerns. A buyer who is seeking an Evo-powered bike should plan to review and prepare to replace the following key items (if the current owner hasn't done so already):

Stator and regulator

Old flooded-type battery

Intake seals

Paper base gaskets (approximately 7.5 hours of labor)

Primary seals

Paper base gaskets (approximately 7.5 hours of labor)

Limited suspension travel and solid-mounted engine equal a rough ride.

Intake seals

Old flooded-type battery

Primary seals

Stator and regulator

Chapter 6

1985 Four-speed Evo Low Rider or Wide Glide

The mid-1980s was a transitional period for Harley-Davidson. The Motor Company returned to private ownership following the 1981 buyout, and the new management moved forward with plans to put the Evolution engine into service. The goal was to introduce it for 1983, but minor teething problems delayed that for another year. Consequently, some 1984 and even several 1985 Big Twin models contained a mixture of engines and transmission combinations that might seem out of whack to enthusiasts today. For instance, early 1984 FXE and FXSB models used outdated Shovelhead engines, with production switching to Evolution engines by year's end.

The swapping wasn't confined to engines only. Chain final drive was used on some models; belt drive on others. Same for transmissions, some models receiving the new five-speed box, while other models were given leftover four-speed transmissions with matching primary assemblies. Harley-Davidson mechanics and tuners referred to those bikes as "parts bin" models, and there seemed to be no absolute rule about what components went on which models.

Among the parts bin specials was the 1985 FXSB Low Rider, a favorite among enthusiasts since its introduction as the FXS during 1977 Daytona Bike Week. The 1977 FXS was the first custom variation on the six-year-old FX theme, a practice of determining new models that Harley-Davidson often follows to this day.

Despite its valued place in the lineup, the 1985 FXSB became a parts-bin bike because much of Harley-Davidson's energy was focused on the FXST Softail and the burgeoning FXR line. Those bikes took advantage of Harley-Davidson's latest technology, including the Evo engine, five-speed transmission, belt drive, and all-new frames for both models. But the FXSB retained the FX frame that originated during the Shovelhead era.

The original FXS Low Rider used a chain drive, but by 1983 Harley engineers converted the bike to belt drive. In the process, the Low Rider picked up its designation as the FXSB; the "B" means belt drive.

And so, for 1985, the FXSB's parts shuffling came to a halt. What greeted customers in Harley-Davidson showrooms was a bike with a seat height slightly less than 26 inches. The drivetrain included the new 80-cubic-inch Evo engine linked to an old four-speed transmission that drove the trademark 16-inch rear wheel via Harley's relatively new belt drive.

In terms of styling, the FXSB had a stubbier fork than that of the FXWG Wide Glide, and its wheelbase was set at 63.5 inches. The exposed battery on the right side identified the Low Rider as having the earlier FX frame, and the stepped seat helped portray the custom-bike image. The bike's redeeming value was its Evolution engine, superior in every way to the Shovelhead that it replaced. As the writers from *Cycle Guide* magazine stated in one of the first road tests of an Evo-powered Harley: "The engine starts easily when cold, and requires only a short warm-up period before the rider can experience the big twin's seductive appeal. That appeal can be summed up in one word: *torque.*"

The 1985 FXSB may have been a parts bin bike, but it retained the heart and soul of a Harley-Davidson motorcycle. And that was important then as it is today.

1985 FXSB Low Rider specifications

Drivetrain

Engine:	Evolution
Layout:	45-degree V-twin
Displacement:	80 cubic inches (1,340 cc)
Cooling:	Air-cooled
Compression ratio:	8.5:1
Fuel system:	Carbureted
Horsepower:	64.0 @ 5,000 rpm
Primary drive:	Chain, 34/46
Transmission:	Four-speed
Final drive:	Belt

Chassis

Fuel capacity:	3.4 gallons
Oil capacity:	3.5 quarts
Wheelbase:	64.7 inches
Weight:	611 pounds (wet)
Seat height (unlade):	25.5 inches

Suspension

Front:	Telescopic fork
Rear:	Twin shocks

Brakes

Front:	1 disc
Rear:	1 disc
Wheels:	19 inches (front), 16 inches (rear)

What they said

"The plain (so to speak) Wide Glide had the older frame... a 21-inch front wheel and rear fender that looked like the like the front fenders chopper guys used to put on the rear...with a V2 engine and good ol' kick start just in case."—Allen Girdler, *Illustrated Harley-Davidson Buyer's Guide*

Parts prices/cost of typical repairs

Parts and Ownership Costs: Typical H-D dealer labor rate = $90/hour

Maintenance item	Action	Interval*	Estimated cost
Air filter	Inspect, service as required		$12.95
Air suspension	Check pressure, operation, and leakage	Annually	
Base gasket	Inspect as necessary		7.5 hours labor $750 total @ dealer
Battery	Check battery and clean connections. Old flooded-type batteries should be immediately replaced.	Annually	
Brake fluid	Check levels and condition	Check level annually. Flush and replace with new fluid every 2 years	
Brake pads and discs	Inspect for wear	Replace as needed	
Clutch	Check adjustment		
Critical fasteners	Check tightness	Every 5,000 miles	
Cruise control	Inspect disengage switch and components	As required	
Drive belt and sprockets	Inspect, adjust belt	Adjustment should be performed by dealer	
Electrical equipment and switches	Check operation		
Engine oil and filter	Replace	Every 5,000 miles	
Fork oil	Replace	Every 10,000 miles	2.5 hours labor $275 total @ dealer
Fuel door and saddlebags	Lubricate hinges and latches	As required	
Fuel lines and fittings	Inspect for leaks	Annually	
Jiffy stand	Inspect and lubricate	Annually	
Oil lines and system	Inspect for leaks	Annually	
Primary chain case lubricant	Replace	Every 10,000 miles	
Spark plugs	Inspect	Replace every 20,000 miles	
Steering head bearings	Lubricate	50,000 miles	
Throttle, brake, clutch controls	Check, adjust, and lubricate		
Tires	Check pressure, inspect tread		
Transmission lubricant	Replace	Every 20,000 miles	
Wheel spokes	Check tightness		
Wheel bearings			.6 hours labor $120 total @ dealer
Three-fluid change	(Crankcase, primary, transmission oils)		.3 hours labor $170 total @ dealer
20,000 mile service	3 fluid change, all req. maint Check spark plugs		$700 total @ dealer

Note: If the bike has been unused and in storage for more than three years, all of these items should receive immediate attention, and key fluids and lubricants should be drained and replaced.

Usability and collectibility ratings

Usability: ★ This is an old-school Harley with a modern engine. The frame dates back to the original Duo-Glide from 1958. It even still has the post for the sprung buddy seat.

Collectibility: ★★★ This bike was an anachronism in 1985 and is even more so today. Although the Softail was no more practical, at least it had proper chopper styling.

Garage Watch
Key items to look for.

Stator and regulator

Old flooded-type battery

Solid-mounted four-speed engine vibrates like a diesel-powered personal massage device.

Evo bikes have many common maintenance concerns. A buyer who is seeking an Evo-powered bike should plan to review and prepare to replace the following key items (if the current owner hasn't done so already):

Stator and regulator

Old flooded-type battery

Intake seals

Paper base gaskets (approximately 7.5 hours of labor)

Primary seals

Intake seals

Primary seals

Paper base gaskets (approximately 7.5 hours of labor)

Chapter 7

1985 to 1990 Four-speed Sportster 883

The entry-level Harley Sportster garnered a great deal of attention in the late 1980s. Yamaha and Honda were selling Viragos and Shadows at very attractive prices, and Harley was struggling to make its Sportsters competitive in the market. In late 1985, Harley hit the Japanese challenge head-on and introduced a radically improved Sportster (sold as a 1986 model). The key to this new Sportster, of course, was the Evolution engine.

Harley had developed an 883-cc Evo that retained the classic look of the Sportster engine, yet shared many common design elements with the 1,338-cc Evo. Most of the key components were now made of aluminum alloy, and the cylinder itself is aluminum with an iron liner. An aluminum top-end replaced the former cast-iron pieces, and the Sportster received an all-new valvetrain, including hydraulic valve lifters and roller tappets. This new top-end was designed with three-piece rocker covers—just like the larger Evo. The three-piece design allowed the removal of the heads and cylinders without removing the entire engine from the bike. The combustion chamber was reshaped, new flat-top pistons were installed, and the engine's combustion cycle was improved using modern computerized analysis of the fuel and airflow.

Power goes to the Sporty's wheel via a standard four-speed transmission. Why only a four-speed? The design of the alloy XL engine placed the alternator inside the primary case behind the diaphragm clutch. As a result, Harley engineers deemed that there was not enough room inside the case for a five-speed gear train. Nonetheless, the transmission's internals were given a healthy dose of quality improvement. New manufacturing techniques improved the quality of the gears and the tolerances, and this resulted in a quieter, smoother, and more durable gearbox.

In keeping with tradition, the 1986 Sportster was a no-frills bike. There was no tool kit or tachometer, and it had only one mirror. The solo seat was thinly padded, there was minimal chrome trim, and paint options were few.

On the road, the Sportster was transformed. Gone were the hand- and body-numbing vibrations from the engine. Noise from the intake, valvetrain, and exhaust were greatly reduced. The suspension was tight now—and the bike handled well! Once into a turn, the chassis settled well and cornering lines were easy to hold. Overall stability was excellent, too, and the stock Dunlop tires were grippy and allowed a rider to take advantage of the Sportster's generous cornering clearances.

Harley finally had a motorcycle that could go head-to-head with the strong Japanese competition. The Evo powertrain was a huge improvement for the Sportster's performance and rideability. The new engine made good power at low revs and accelerated the Sportster with authority. Much of the previous engine's vibrations were eliminated, making the Sportster more comfortable to ride for extended distances. Best of all, this Harley Goodness came at the very reasonable MSRP of $3,995. It was a deal that would revive Harley's entry-level lineup and set the stage to pull new riders into the Harley fold.

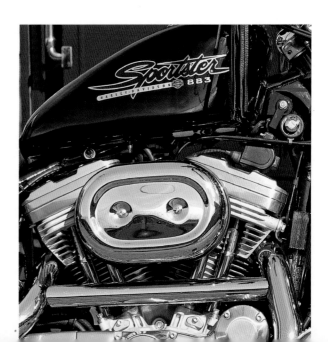

1986 XLH-883 specifications

Drivetrain
Engine:	Evolution
Layout:	45-degree V-twin
Displacement:	54 cubic inches (883 cc)
Cooling:	Air-cooled
Compression ratio:	9.0:1
Fuel system:	Carburetor
Horsepower:	42.0 brake horsepower @ 6,000 rpm
Primary drive:	Chain
Transmission:	Four-speed
Final drive:	Chain

Chassis
Fuel capacity:	2.25 gallons
Wheelbase:	60 inches
Weight:	478 pounds (wet)
Seat height (unlade):	30 inches

Suspension
Front:	Telescopic fork
Rear:	Twin shocks, swingarm

Brakes
Front:	1 disc
Rear:	1 disc
Wheels:	19 inches (front), 16 inches (rear)

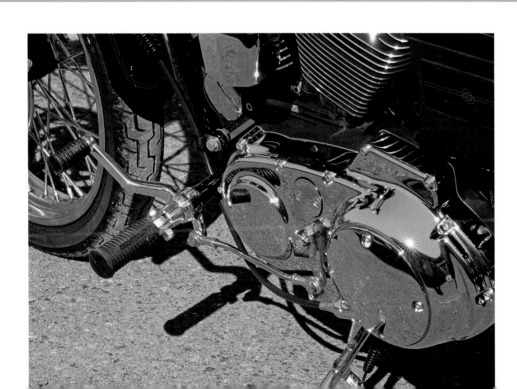

Parts prices/cost of typical repairs

Parts and Ownership Costs: Typical H-D dealer labor rate = $90/hour

Maintenance item	Action	Interval*	Estimated cost
Air filter	Inspect, service as required		$12.95
Air suspension	Check pressure, operation, and leakage	Annually	
Base gasket	Inspect as necessary		7.5 hours labor $750 total @ dealer
Battery	Check battery and clean connections. Old flooded-type batteries should be immediately replaced.	Annually	
Brake fluid	Check levels and condition	Check level annually. Flush and replace with new fluid every 2 years	
Brake pads and discs	Inspect for wear	Replace as needed	
Clutch	Check adjustment		
Critical fasteners	Check tightness	Every 5,000 miles	
Cruise control	Inspect disengage switch and components	As required	
Drive belt and sprockets	Inspect, adjust belt	Adjustment should be performed by dealer	
Electrical equipment and switches	Check operation		
Engine oil and filter	Replace	Every 5,000 miles	
Fork oil	Replace	Every 10,000 miles	2.5 hours labor $275 total @ dealer
Fuel door and saddlebags	Lubricate hinges and latches	As required	
Fuel lines and fittings	Inspect for leaks	Annually	
Jiffy stand	Inspect and lubricate	Annually	
Oil lines and system	Inspect for leaks	Annually	
Primary chain case lubricant	Replace	Every 10,000 miles	
Spark plugs	Inspect	Replace every 20,000 miles	
Steering head bearings	Lubricate	50,000 miles	
Throttle, brake, clutch controls	Check, adjust, and lubricate		
Tires	Check pressure, inspect tread		
Transmission lubricant	Replace	Every 20,000 miles	
Wheel spokes	Check tightness		
Wheel bearings			.6 hours labor $120 total @ dealer
Three-fluid change	(Crankcase, primary, transmission oils)		.3 hours labor $170 total @ dealer
20,000 mile service	3 fluid change, all req. maint Check spark plugs		$700 total @ dealer

Note: If the bike has been unused and in storage for more than three years, all of these items should receive immediate attention, and key fluids and lubricants should be drained and replaced.

What they said

"A four-speed transmission might sound skimpy on other motorcycles but even the smallest of Harley's big-inch twins makes more than enough low-speed urge to provide the kind of wide range power that comfortably spans several gearbox ratios at any given road speed. The XLH electric-starts readily and is rolling while other bikes are still trying to wipe the sleep out of their eyes. Once fired, the XLH power plant announces that internal combustion is spoken here, not only with its big-V cadence but also with vibration that reaches you through bars, pegs and saddle. The vibes are subdued enough not to grate on you unless you spend the whole day aboard, but you'll never wonder if you're riding an electric motor. The 53.8-cubic-inch engine can propel the 487-pound (wet weight) XLH through the quarter mile in 13.95 seconds at 93.8 mph and delivers over 50 miles per gallon on the highway. You'll come to appreciate the good fuel mileage in a hurry with the stylishly small 2.3-gallon fuel tank."
—*Motorcyclist*, March, 1990 (1990 XLH-883)

"Besides price, the Sportster has its looks going for it. As it has done sine its inception in 1957, the Sporty displays the classic Harley image of a simple motorcycle with a large, well-detailed V-Twin engine dominating the proceedings. To many people, the Sportster is just what a motorcycle should look like.

But there are detractions. On the road, even at normal highway speeds, the Harley's booming, shaking, solidly mounted engine sends its power impulses into the rider's body and soul. Its rear view mirrors keep time with the engine's power cycles, turning reflected images into a blur. The bike's fork does a fair job of smoothing out rough roads, but the rear suspension isn't much better than a hardtail—bumps are transmitted directly to the rider's spine, Furthermore, the seat's padding (our test bike was fitted with an optional duel seat) is thin and quickly packs into a useless butt punisher. Fuel range, topped-up to bone-dry, is less than 100 miles, and the bike's forward mounted footpegs didn't make too many friends among our test riders."
—*Cycle World*, July, 1990

"The Evolution Sportster is the most modern Harley yet, offering the advantages of the Evolution engine—precision, efficiency, smoother and more consistent operation, and greatly reduced maintenance—with Harley-Davidson's latest technology for transmission, clutch, etc."—*Motorcyclist* (1986 XLH-883)

Usability and collectibility ratings

Usability: ★★ Many people complain about the small gas tank on the Sportsters from this era. Anyone who has ridden one any distance will realize the importance of stopping every 70 or 80 miles.

Collectibility: ★★ Harley sold these things by the tens of thousands. They are far too common to ever be collectible.

Recalls and service bulletins

The 1987–90 XLH bikes were recalled for a possible failure of the upper mounting bolt for the front brake caliper. The failure of this mounting bolt could cause the bolt to become lodged in the front wheel and cause a lockup.

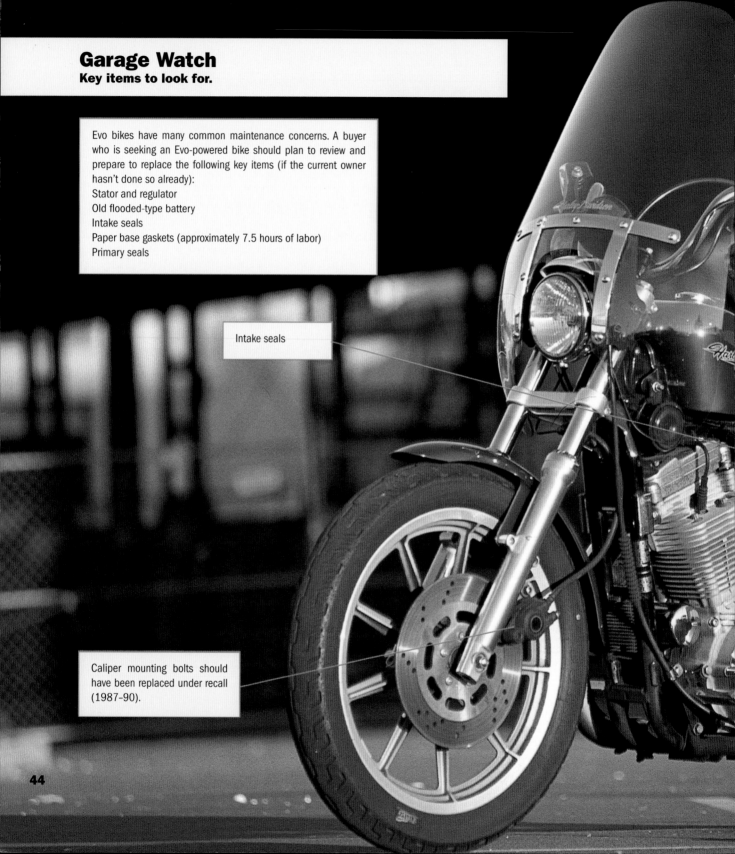

Garage Watch
Key items to look for.

Evo bikes have many common maintenance concerns. A buyer who is seeking an Evo-powered bike should plan to review and prepare to replace the following key items (if the current owner hasn't done so already):

Stator and regulator

Old flooded-type battery

Intake seals

Paper base gaskets (approximately 7.5 hours of labor)

Primary seals

Intake seals

Caliper mounting bolts should have been replaced under recall (1987–90).

The '86- onward Sportster 883s were transformed into quieter, less vibrating and better-handling machines than their predecessors, and were quite affordable with an MSRP of around $4,000.

Old flooded-type battery

Primary seals

Stator and regulator

Paper base gaskets (approximately 7.5 hours of labor)

Chapter 8

1985 to 1986 XLH1100 and 1988 to 1990 Four-speed XLH1200 Sportster

Harley buyers typically fall into two groups, those who appreciate new styling and modernization and those who want only a "traditional" Harley-Davidson. Harley was clearly targeting the 883 at the "modern" Harley buyers. Its style and performance were developed to compete with the growing competition from Honda and Yamaha. The XLH1100 was aimed at the "traditional" Harley buyer, one who was seeking a less aggressive attitude and a more fully featured bike than was found on the basic 883.

The XLH1100 and the XLH883 have much in common. The bikes are built on the same rigid-mount chassis, and their engines share some common core pieces. The 1100 is virtually a bored-out version of the 883, and despite larger valves, it shares the same cylinder head design and has hydraulic lifters. Its cylinders are aluminum alloy with iron liners. The stroke is the same as the 883, and the compression ratio is identical at 9.0:1. The Keihin 34-millimeter carburetor, ignition, clutch, and final drive are shared also. Like the 883, the 1100 has a four-speed transmission and chain drive. Curb weights are almost the same too. Cost considerations precluded the use of rubber engine mounts and five-speed belt final drives on both of these Sportsters.

While they are indeed similar bikes, the 883 and the 1100 differ in their styling, riding position, power, and amenities. The 883 is a stripped-down, minimalist bike—one mirror, no tachometer, a solo seat—and a price to match. The 1100 is clearly a step up in comfort and style. From its wraparound front fender to its traditional pullback bar and stepped two-up saddle, the 1100 has more features and comfort than the basic 883.

The bigger engine is significant too. The 1100 is notably stronger than the 883, making more horsepower and torque through the entire powerband. The four-speed transmission and diaphragm clutch work well, though riders will find that shifts require deliberate pressure on the lever to execute consistent shifts without finding false neutral. Gear spacing in the four-speed transmission is good for urban riding, though there is a disproportionately wide spacing between the third and fourth ratios.

The Showa suspension at the front and rear is tuned for comfort and compliance, and it is well-suited to solo riding. Despite this suspension tuning, the 1100 has ample cornering clearance and can be fun for spirited riding in the twisties. The raked front end geometry makes steering slower, but tire traction is ample and the Sportster can handle moderately spirited riding without complaint. The Sportster also tracks very well in a straight line and is stable at nominal highway speeds. Note, however, that there is only 3.3 inches of travel in the rear suspension, and ride quality is not great for two-up riding of any significant distance. Braking is also a weaker point, with the single-piston front and rear discs barely adequate for a bike of this weight and power.

The Sportsters were again in the spotlight in 1988. That year, the Sportster's 1100 mill was punched out to displace a full 1,200 cc (74 cubic inches). That number 74 may ring a bell. It's the same displacement that Harley's Big Twins had for many years. Harley's Sportster was getting some serious motivation, and it was difficult for Big Twin riders to call a 1200 Sportster a "girl's bike." The Evo in the Sportster got improvements that were not immediately visible from the outside. New cams and a 40-millimeter CV carburetor improved the engine's breathing and fuel intake (this carburetor was also installed on the 883 Sportsters). The XL1200 gained a few pounds over its predecessor, the 1100, but it also gained about 10 percent more horsepower. Harley was taking the fierce Japanese competition seriously, and the move to a 1,200-cc mill made the Sportster a contender in the increasingly crowded cruiser marketplace of the late 1980s.

The XLH1100 and XLH1200 Sportsters succeed in their mission as a step up from the very basic 883. Even today they still represent a good value for the money.

1986 XLH100 specifications

Drivetrain

Engine:	Evolution
Layout:	45-degree V-twin
Displacement:	67 cubic inches (1,101 cc)
Cooling:	Air-cooled
Compression ratio:	9.0:1
Fuel system:	Carburetor
Horsepower:	53.0 brake horsepower @ 6,000 rpm
Primary drive:	Chain
Transmission:	Four-speed
Final drive:	Chain

Chassis

Fuel capacity:	2.25 gallons
Wheelbase:	60.0 inches
Weight:	494 pounds (wet)
Seat height (unlade):	30 inches

Suspension

Front:	Telescopic fork, 35 millimeters
Rear:	Twin shocks, swingarm, 76-millimeter wheel travel

Brakes

Front:	1 disc
Rear:	1 disc
Wheels:	19 inches (front), 16 inches (rear)

Parts prices/cost of typical repairs

Parts and Ownership Costs: Typical H-D dealer labor rate = $90/hour

Maintenance item	Action	Interval*	Estimated cost
Air filter	Inspect, service as required		$12.95
Air suspension	Check pressure, operation, and leakage	Annually	
Base gasket	Inspect as necessary		7.5 hours labor $750 total @ dealer
Battery	Check battery and clean connections. Old flooded-type batteries should be immediately replaced.	Annually	
Brake fluid	Check levels and condition	Check level annually. Flush and replace with new fluid every 2 years	
Brake pads and discs	Inspect for wear	Replace as needed	
Clutch	Check adjustment		
Critical fasteners	Check tightness	Every 5,000 miles	
Cruise control	Inspect disengage switch and components	As required	
Drive belt and sprockets	Inspect, adjust belt	Adjustment should be performed by dealer	
Electrical equipment and switches	Check operation		
Engine oil and filter	Replace	Every 5,000 miles	
Fork oil	Replace	Every 10,000 miles	2.5 hours labor $275 total @ dealer
Fuel door and saddlebags	Lubricate hinges and latches	As required	
Fuel lines and fittings	Inspect for leaks	Annually	
Jiffy stand	Inspect and lubricate	Annually	
Oil lines and system	Inspect for leaks	Annually	
Primary chain case lubricant	Replace	Every 10,000 miles	
Spark plugs	Inspect	Replace every 20,000 miles	
Steering head bearings	Lubricate	50,000 miles	
Throttle, brake, clutch controls	Check, adjust, and lubricate		
Tires	Check pressure, inspect tread		
Transmission lubricant	Replace	Every 20,000 miles	
Wheel spokes	Check tightness		
Wheel bearings			.6 hours labor $120 total @ dealer
Three-fluid change	(Crankcase, primary, transmission oils)		.3 hours labor $170 total @ dealer
20,000 mile service	3 fluid change, all req. maint Check spark plugs		$700 total @ dealer

Note: If the bike has been unused and in storage for more than three years, all of these items should receive immediate attention, and key fluids and lubricants should be drained and replaced.

What they said

"Not only does it incorporate some fairly extensive changes in its 45-degree V-Twin engine, it also is the largest-displacement Sportster ever built, and one of the fastest. But beneath it all, the 1100 still is a traditional H-D through and through." —*Cycle World* (1986 XLH1100)

"Current engineering at Harley has transformed the 1100 into a stronger, more polished product than past Sportsters, but anyone familiar with the breed will recognize certain enduring traits: Although modern technology at Harley runs to rubber-mounted engines, belt drive, and five-speed transmissions—the function of all this technology intended to isolate the rider from the bump and grind of a big V-twin while he enjoys its engaging mechanical presence—the 1100, like the original Sportster, attains through its solid-mounted, four-speed, chain-drive engine an almost historic intensity. In these days of glass-smooth powerplants and shift levers that click into gear like a ballpoint pen, the 1100 is a high-effort ride." —*Cycle*, May 1987 (1987 XLH1100)

"Even though they are almost identical motorcycles, I think I like the 883 better, mostly because it's smoother. I wish one Evolution Sportster had a five-speed and a saddle good for more than 45 minutes. A five-speed would set the 1100 further apart from the 883 and make it more interesting."—*Motorcyclist* (1986 XLH1100)

"Seventy-four cub inches seems to be a magic number for Harley. I'd been riding another big V-twin before I rode the Sportster, but even though it was slower and not as smooth as that 1500, I preferred the way the biggest Sportster worked and felt. The Sportster is unique. It's not a cruiser. It's not a standard. It's not a Musclebike. It's a Sportster: not too radical, not too plain, not horrendously fast and certainly not in step with the beat of someone else's drum. The 1200 seems to be the most independently minded Sporty in a long time, and in many ways I like it the best of any of Harley's "little" bikes. I'd want to change the turn-signal controls, shocks and saddle if I bought one, but I like the chassis a lot. The front suspension, front bake, wide-angle mirrors and feel of the throttle and clutch were all immediately noticeable improvements when I rode the 1200. I like the added power too, but I wish it came with the smoothness of the 883 mill. Even so, it should tempt a lot of 883 owners to trade up."— *Motorcyclist*, October, 1987 (1988 XLH1200)

Usability and collectibility ratings

Usability: ★★★ The 1100 Sportsters were a little smoother and quite a bit more powerful than their 883 siblings. The 1200 Sportsters were even better than the 1100s.

Collectibility: ★★★ The 1100 rates three stars for its rarity; the 1200 just two because it was produced in much higher numbers.

Recalls and service bulletins

The 1987–90 XLH bikes were recalled for a possible failure of the upper mounting bolt for the front brake caliper, which could become lodged in the front wheel and cause a lockup.

Garage Watch
Key items to look for.

Evo bikes have many common maintenance concerns. A buyer who is seeking an Evo-powered bike should plan to review and prepare to replace the following key items (if the current owner hasn't done so already):
Stator and regulator
Old flooded-type battery
Intake seals
Paper base gaskets (approximately 7.5 hours of labor)
Primary seals

Old flooded-type battery

Stator and regulator

Intake seals

Primary seals

Caliper mounting bolt should have been replaced under recall (1987–90).

Paper base gaskets (approximately 7.5 hours of labor)

Mounting a Springer suspension on the FXSTS was an epic styling move by Willie G. This is a front-suspension design that hadn't been seen on a production Harley since 1949. Its key features are two spring towers that protrude above the fork crown with a damper mounted in front. This retro suspension was mated to the now-proven Softail chassis and its rigid-mounted Big Twin. The result: an instant modern classic.

The concept of a Springer was not new within the Harley culture, and once the idea was put onto the table, everybody involved in design, engineering, and manufacturing agreed that it would ultimately be a fantastic bike. But this new/old suspension system came at a cost. It created a huge task for Harley's engineers. They had to bring the design forward almost 40 years, meeting the safety and durability requirements of a modern motorcycle.

Using computer-aided design systems and other modern design tools, Harley's engineers built a Springer front end that looked authentic, provided ample suspension travel, integrated a front disc brake, and had a modern service interval. The keystone piece to the Springer suspension is its bearings. These hemispherical Teflon bearings are essentially half of a conventional ball joint, located on each side of the rigid fork legs. Each bearing's play can be easily adjusted when the front wheel is removed, and Harley recommends doing this on a 10,000-mile interval.

This impressively re-created Springer suspension was mounted to the Softail frame, resulting in the FXSTS Springer Softail. The Softail is the perfect bike to accommodate the Springer suspension. After all, its rear suspension mimics the look of the hardtails of yore. The addition of the Springer front suspension brings the Softail's styling full circle.

The geometry of a Springer's suspension has inherent design advantages too. A Springer doesn't "dive" under hard braking like a telescopic suspension does, and Harley engineers designed the Springer to offer 4 inches of travel, which is comparable to the travel of a contemporary telescopic fork. Telescopic forks have a *lot* of friction when mounted at radical rake angles. The "bending" loads on the front end cause the friction, which can create a kink in the fork tube. To counter this, bikes with long, raked front ends must use stout telescopic fork tubes (today's Softail Rocker C uses 49-millimeter tubes).

On the road, the Springer rides well. Despite the added weight of the front suspension, the Springer turns with little effort, and the highway ride is pleasantly damped. The Softail rear suspension offers only 3.4 inches of travel, but this is acceptable for most riding situations that a Springer owner will likely encounter. The Springer's rigid-mounted Evo shakes and throbs, but it is comfortable at cruising revs and it is mated to a five-speed transmission and belt final drive. The result is a Softail that can handle some curves, but is truly tailored for the smooth, open road.

Willie G. reached back into Harley's history and created a masterpiece of styling and unintentional innovation. The Springer Softail is as classic as classic Harleys get, and 1988 Springers are among the most collectible Harleys of the modern era.

1988 FXSTS Springer Softail specifications

Drivetrain

Engine:	Evolution
Layout:	45-degree V-twin
Displacement:	80 cubic inches (1,340 cc)
Cooling:	Air-cooled
Compression ratio:	8.5:1
Fuel system:	Carburetor
Horsepower:	58.0 brake horsepower @ 5,000 rpm
Primary drive:	Chain
Transmission:	Five-speed
Final drive:	Belt

Chassis

Fuel capacity:	5.2 gallons
Wheelbase:	64.0 inches
Weight:	649 pounds (wet)
Seat height (unlade):	26.3 inches

Suspension

Front:	Harley-Davidson Springer, one Monroe damper, 4.0-inch wheel travel
Rear:	Twin shocks, 3.4-inch wheel travel

Brakes

Front:	1 disc
Rear:	1 disc
Wheels:	21 inches (front), 16 inches (rear)

What they said

"The whole idea of this Springer is hilarious. I laughed and shook my head when I heard that the rumors were true, that Harley was actually going to build the thing. . . . Someone may buy a Springer because of its looks, but he'll also be getting something that works. Nice going, H-D, you pulled it off."—*Motorcyclist*, July, 1988 (1988 FXSTS)

"Harley will make 1,300 of these machines, all identically painted, all with the 85th anniversary graphics on their tanks and high-riding front fenders. At $10,695, only $850 more than an FXSTC, they may be legitimate bargains, pukka collectors' items, and motorcycles to be polished and treasured for years to come. All that, and they work better too."—*Motorcyclist*, July, 1988 (1988 FXSTS)

"Harley's engineers didn't let the front-suspension revolution start without them. However, even though this back-to-the-future front fork may work a bit better than a telescopic design, I am less convinced that it accomplished its primary mission. In other words, I think the springer fork is kind of ugly, with those exposed springs, the big damper and the almost dirt-bike-like front-fender clearance.

Still, if you can get a reworked design of an ancient nontelescopic design to work better than a telescoping legs we are forced to put up with on most of the rest of the world's current motorcycles, imagine what could happen if somebody worked up an all-new design. How do you feel when a nostalgic piece like this has a better fork design than your high-tech sport bike?"—*Motorcyclist*, July, 1988 (1988 FXSTS)

Parts prices/cost of typical repairs

Parts and Ownership Costs: Typical H-D dealer labor rate = $90/hour

Maintenance item	Action	Interval*	Estimated cost
Air filter	Inspect, service as required		$12.95
Air suspension	Check pressure, operation, and leakage	Annually	
Base gasket	Inspect as necessary		7.5 hours labor $750 total @ dealer
Battery	Check battery and clean connections. Old flooded-type batteries should be immediately replaced.	Annually	
Brake fluid	Check levels and condition	Check level annually. Flush and replace with new fluid every 2 years	
Brake pads and discs	Inspect for wear	Replace as needed	
Clutch	Check adjustment		
Critical fasteners	Check tightness	Every 5,000 miles	
Cruise control	Inspect disengage switch and components	As required	
Drive belt and sprockets	Inspect, adjust belt	Adjustment should be performed by dealer	
Electrical equipment and switches	Check operation		
Engine oil and filter	Replace	Every 5,000 miles	
Fork oil	Replace	Every 10,000 miles	2.5 hours labor $275 total @ dealer
Fuel door and saddlebags	Lubricate hinges and latches	As required	
Fuel lines and fittings	Inspect for leaks	Annually	
Jiffy stand	Inspect and lubricate	Annually	
Oil lines and system	Inspect for leaks	Annually	
Primary chain case lubricant	Replace	Every 10,000 miles	
Spark plugs	Inspect	Replace every 20,000 miles	
Steering head bearings	Lubricate	50,000 miles	
Throttle, brake, clutch controls	Check, adjust, and lubricate		
Tires	Check pressure, inspect tread		
Transmission lubricant	Replace	Every 20,000 miles	
Wheel spokes	Check tightness		
Wheel bearings			.6 hours labor $120 total @ dealer
Three-fluid change	(Crankcase, primary, transmission oils)		.3 hours labor $170 total @ dealer
20,000 mile service	3 fluid change, all req. maint Check spark plugs		$700 total @ dealer

Note: If the bike has been unused and in storage for more than three years, all of these items should receive immediate attention, and key fluids and lubricants should be drained and replaced.

Usability and collectibility ratings

Usability: ★★★ The funky springer front end actually performed better than the hydraulic unit on lesser Softails.

Collectibility: ★★★★ The original Springer never caught on, mostly because the high-mounted fender looked like it had been pilfered from a motocross bike. A redesign fixed the problem, but the bike was never sold in huge numbers.

Recalls and service bulletins

The 1988 FXSTS Softail Springers were subject to a recall to replace a front brake caliper bolt that had the potential to come loose and cause brake failure.

The 1989–90 Softail Springers were recalled for the possible failure of rear brake hydraulic lines. Leaks could cause a loss of braking power and are a safety concern.

The 1989–92 Softail Springers were recalled to replace a starter relay that could potentially short circuit. If the relay overheats and the circuit shorts out, it could cause a fire in the relay that could spread to other parts of the motorcycle.

Garage Watch

Key items to look for.

Evo bikes have many common maintenance concerns. A buyer who is seeking an Evo-powered bike should plan to review and prepare to replace the following key items (if the current owner hasn't done so already):

Stator and regulator

Old flooded-type battery

Intake seals

Paper base gaskets (approximately 7.5 hours of labor)

Primary seals

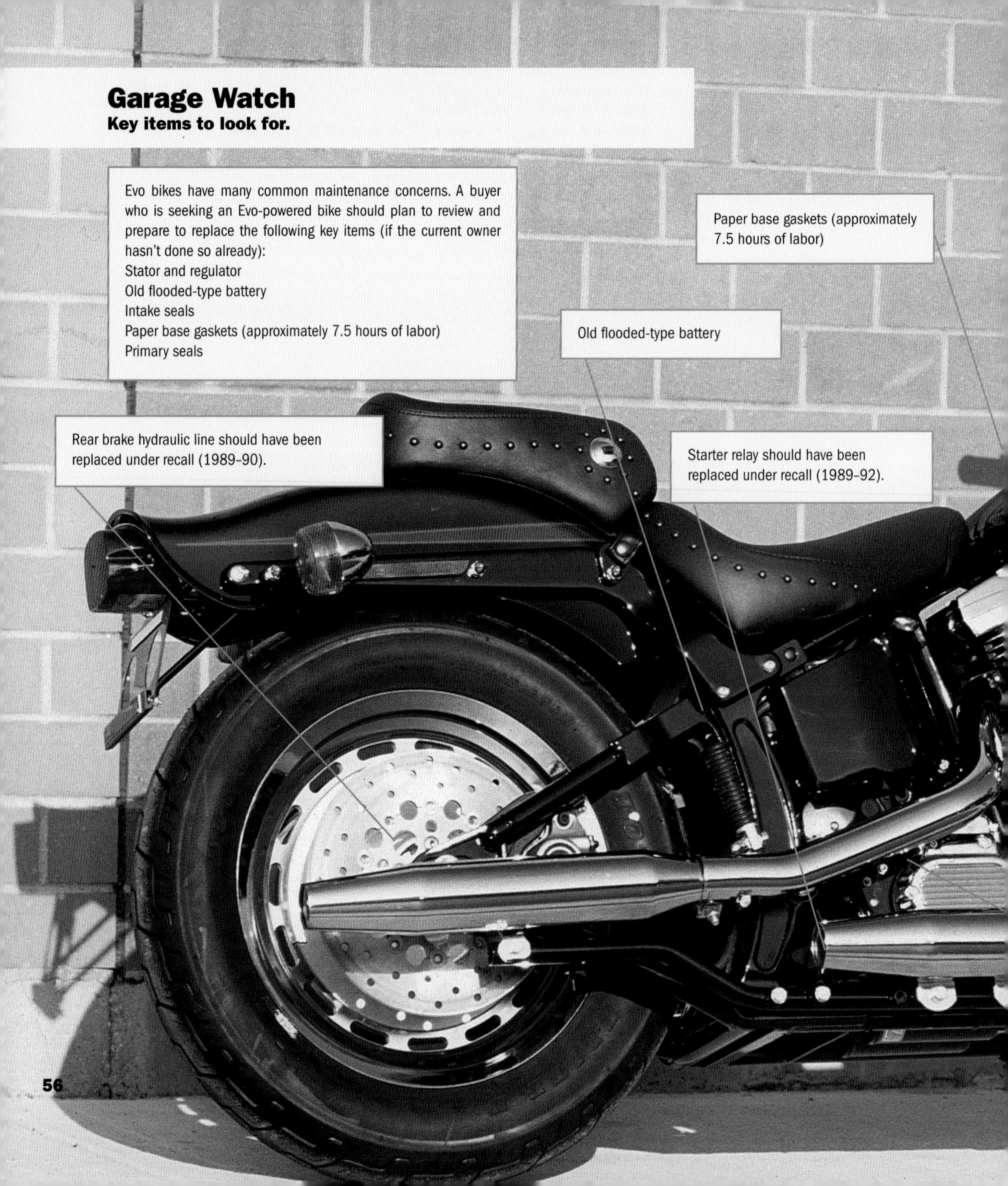

Paper base gaskets (approximately 7.5 hours of labor)

Old flooded-type battery

Rear brake hydraulic line should have been replaced under recall (1989–90).

Starter relay should have been replaced under recall (1989–92).

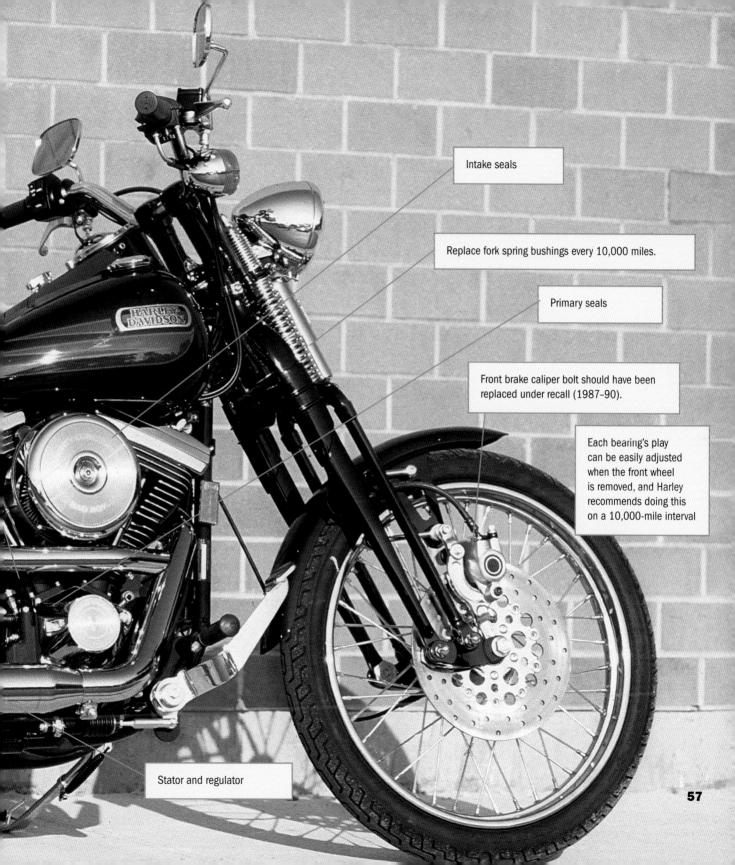

Intake seals

Replace fork spring bushings every 10,000 miles.

Primary seals

Front brake caliper bolt should have been replaced under recall (1987–90).

Each bearing's play can be easily adjusted when the front wheel is removed, and Harley recommends doing this on a 10,000-mile interval

Stator and regulator

Chapter 10

1987 to 1999 FLSTC Heritage Softail Classic

In 1986, Willie G. wanted to expand on the Softail lineup. The Softail chassis had enormous potential, and Willie G. viewed it as a canvas upon which to develop an entirely new family of Harleys. The Softail, with its hardtail look, was clean and decidedly retro. Yet it disguised a modern rear suspension that allowed the Softail to handle well and be comfortable to ride for extended distances.

The Heritage Softail was the result of Willie G.'s creative inspiration to mate the Softail chassis with a front suspension that resembled that of the famous Hydra Glide of 1949–57. The most prominent design features of the Hydra Glide are intact on the Heritage: the stout telescopic fork tubes and the skirted front fender. Of course, the Softail suspension gives the Heritage an authentic hardtail appearance, and the bike retains the classic proportions and the direct design "line" that runs from the rear axle hub to the steering head. The Heritage Softail's styling made the bike an instant sales success, and it quickly ranked near the top of Harley's sales charts, a status it has held consistently for the past 20 years.

The FLSTC Heritage Softail Classic is the sibling of the enormously successful Heritage Softail. Introduced in 1986, the Heritage Softail Classic is a more luxurious version of the stylish Heritage Softail. It has amenities that make it a more comfortable long-distance bike and enhance its classic style. It's easy to spot a Heritage Softail Classic. The windshield and soft leather saddlebags are an easy giveaway, and the Heritage Softail Classic retains the bright spoked wheels and bright headlight nacelle that glisten in the sun on long, sunny highway rides. Like all Softails, the Heritage is powered by the 80-cubic-inch Evo mated to a five-speed transmission with a belt final drive.

Adding a windshield and some soft bags to the Heritage Softail transformed the bike into a versatile light-duty touring machine. The riding position of the Softail is comfortable, with an easy reach to the bars and nice, broad floorboards that allow the rider to adjust positions easily during a long haul in the saddle. The stepped saddle is broad and soft and has studs and tassels for added detail. The Heritage has an ample pillion pad for a passenger, and a standard backrest further enhances the passenger's comfort. Both the rider and passenger will appreciate the expansive windshield as the miles roll by.

On the highway, the Heritage is in its element. The Evo has plenty of power to cruise highways at reasonable velocities, even when riding two-up. The bike tracks well and its steering is nimble and light, belying the bulk of the stout front forks. When pushed in the corners, the Heritage will shower the roadway with sparks, but that's not what this bike is all about. It's a comfortable cruiser that can easily double as a touring mount without missing a beat.

The Heritage Softail is probably Harley's most versatile motorcycle. It's a great cruiser that has the comfort and capacity to handle long trips with ease. It's no wonder that it has been one of Harley's most versatile and successful motorcycles of the past 20 years.

1989 FLSTC specifications

Drivetrain

Engine:	Evolution
Layout:	45-degree V-twin
Displacement:	80 cubic inches (1,339 cc)
Cooling:	Air-cooled
Compression ratio:	8.5:1
Fuel system:	Carburetor
Horsepower:	58.0 brake horsepower @ 5,000 rpm
Primary drive:	Chain
Transmission:	Five-speed
Final drive:	Belt

Chassis

Fuel capacity:	4.2 gallons
Wheelbase:	64.5 inches
Weight:	657 pounds (wet)
Seat height (unlade):	25.4 inches

Suspension

Front:	Telescopic forks
Rear:	Twin shocks, 3.4-inch wheel travel

Brakes

Front:	1 disc
Rear:	1 disc
Wheels:	16 inches (front), 16 inches (rear)

What they said

"Motorcycles are beginning to look a lot alike these days, which is why this Harley is such an aesthetically pleasant change of pace. A trip to the grocery store quickly turns into a motorcycling history lesson for the younger set, while folk who remember the '50s just gaze with respect. Be sure to keep it hidden from your girl friend, though. One look and she'll suddenly insist on wearing bobby socks, saddle shoes, a poodle skirt and your old varsity sweater to the movies on Saturday night. Any bike that sparks enthusiasm like that from women is my kind of machine.

'Hey, Julie, I've got a motorcycle you've just got to see.'"—*Motorcyclist*, December, 1986 (1987 FLSTC)

"That retro-styling hit new heights in 1986 when the Heritage Softail debuted, looking for all the world like a 1949 Hydra-Glide that had escaped from a museum. The Heritage Softail Classic, fitted with old-style leather saddlebags and windshield, is perhaps the most complete expression of nostalgia ever mass produced."—*Cycle World*, September, 1993

"The most elegant Harley-Davidson of its generation."—*Cycle* (1986 FLSTC)

Parts prices/cost of typical repairs

Parts and Ownership Costs: Typical H-D dealer labor rate = $90/hour

Maintenance item	Action	Interval*	Estimated cost
Air filter	Inspect, service as required		$12.95
Air suspension	Check pressure, operation, and leakage	Annually	
Base gasket	Inspect as necessary		7.5 hours labor $750 total @ dealer
Battery	Check battery and clean connections. Old flooded-type batteries should be immediately replaced.	Annually	
Brake fluid	Check levels and condition	Check level annually. Flush and replace with new fluid every 2 years	
Brake pads and discs	Inspect for wear	Replace as needed	
Clutch	Check adjustment		
Critical fasteners	Check tightness	Every 5,000 miles	
Cruise control	Inspect disengage switch and components	As required	
Drive belt and sprockets	Inspect, adjust belt	Adjustment should be performed by dealer	
Electrical equipment and switches	Check operation		
Engine oil and filter	Replace	Every 5,000 miles	
Fork oil	Replace	Every 10,000 miles	2.5 hours labor $275 total @ dealer
Fuel door and saddlebags	Lubricate hinges and latches	As required	
Fuel lines and fittings	Inspect for leaks	Annually	
Jiffy stand	Inspect and lubricate	Annually	
Oil lines and system	Inspect for leaks	Annually	
Primary chain case lubricant	Replace	Every 10,000 miles	
Spark plugs	Inspect	Replace every 20,000 miles	
Steering head bearings	Lubricate	50,000 miles	
Throttle, brake, clutch controls	Check, adjust, and lubricate		
Tires	Check pressure, inspect tread		
Transmission lubricant	Replace	Every 20,000 miles	
Wheel spokes	Check tightness		
Wheel bearings			.6 hours labor $120 total @ dealer
Three-fluid change	(Crankcase, primary, transmission oils)		.3 hours labor $170 total @ dealer
20,000 mile service	3 fluid change, all req. maint Check spark plugs		$700 total @ dealer

Note: If the bike has been unused and in storage for more than three years, all of these items should receive immediate attention, and key fluids and lubricants should be drained and replaced.

Usability and collectibility ratings

Usability: ★★★ These are adequate for putting around town. If you're not in any particular hurry, you can even putt across the country.

Collectibility: ★★★★★ The original Heritage has to rank as one of the most collectible Harleys from the post-Shovel era.

Recalls and service bulletins

The 1989–1992 Heritage Softails were recalled to replace a starter relay that could potentially short circuit. If the relay overheats and the circuit shorts out, it could cause a fire that could spread to other parts of the motorcycle. The 1999 Heritage Softails were built with a fuel tank vent fitting that could potentially be plugged. This allows the carburetor to overflow fuel and could lead to a fire.

Garage Watch
Key items to look for.

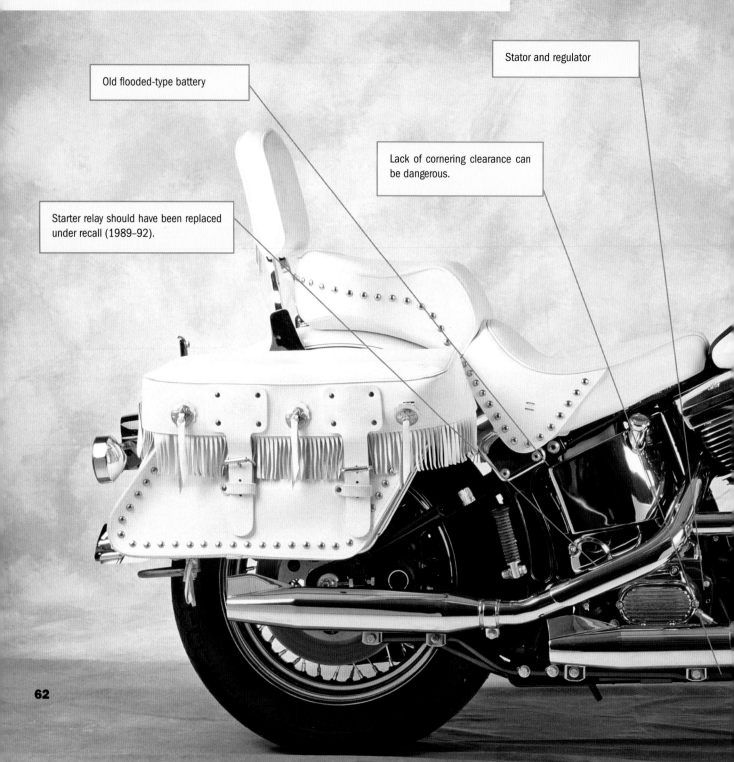

Stator and regulator

Old flooded-type battery

Lack of cornering clearance can be dangerous.

Starter relay should have been replaced under recall (1989–92).

Evo bikes have many common maintenance concerns. A buyer who is seeking an Evo-powered bike should plan to review and prepare to replace the following key items (if the current owner hasn't done so already):
Stator and regulator
Old flooded-type battery
Intake seals
Paper base gaskets (approximately 7.5 hours of labor)
Primary seals

Intake seals

Primary seals

Paper base gaskets (approximately 7.5 hours of labor)

The Fat Boy is the quintessential Harley of the 1990s. Harley had expanded the Softail lineup through the late 1980s, and in 1990 the Motor Company gave the green light to yet another model that would become a blockbuster sales success. The FLSTF Fat Boy arrived, and its modern, sleek, industrial styling cues would make it a dramatic counterpoint to the retro-flavored Springer and Heritage Softails.

The Fat Boy was, of course, built on the Softail chassis, and it had a lot in common with the Heritage Softail. Dual shocks were concealed under the engine, damping impacts that travel through the extended triangular swingarm. Big telescopic forks reminiscent of the Hydra Glide are out front, and the floorboards, seat, and handlebars will feel familiar to riders of the Heritage.

The Fat Boy differs from the Heritage in its styling cues. The Heritage is festooned with retro bits: conchos, studs on the saddle, and a studded set of saddlebags. The Fat Boy is cleaner, notable for its more modern, industrial styling. The front fender is bobbed, flared, and virtually devoid of chrome and trim. The front suspension is exposed and stripped down. The big aluminum fork tubes meet at the triples, which appear to have been hewn from a solid block of billet aluminum. Only a single, round headlight is mounted on the triples, with the turn signals cleverly mounted on the handlebars, beneath the brake and clutch master cylinders. Moving back, the Fat Boy's solo saddle, over and under shotgun exhaust, and clean fender lines give the bike a streamlined profile.

It's difficult to overstate the impact that the Fat Boy had on the overall cruiser market. The bike's clean lines and formidable profile drew stares wherever it was parked. This was a modern interpretation of a custom FL from the 1950s pulled forward to the 1990s. Even Hollywood took note, and the Fat Boy was Schwarzenegger's mount in the 1991 blockbuster film *Terminator 2*. With its powerful stance and clean lines, the Fat Boy was always the center of attention.

Riding the Fat Boy was a visceral experience. There were no fairings to protect the rider from the elements and no oversized two-up saddle, either. The rider sits behind the wide bars on the solo seat, feet perched forward on the running boards and facing into the wind. Fire up the Big Twin (you'll need to use the enrichener when the engine's cold), and the rigid-mounted engine comes to life easily. Rigid-mounted Big Twins will definitely send vibrations to the rider through the bars, seat, and floorboards, and the Fat One is no exception. You don't need a tachometer to know the engine is running.

Once warmed and moving, the Fat Boy is a solid-feeling motorcycle. The engine smoothes out, and the transmission shifts cleanly, albeit with significant effort at the heel-toe shift lever. The Softail suspension is firm but keeps the highway ride comfortable. The solo seat is well-shaped and comfortable for up to 100 miles at a stretch. Beyond that, the rider will probably want to get off the road for a break, as the stiff suspension and lack of weather protection take their toll.

The Fat Boy proved to be a renaissance event in American motorcycle styling. Its minimalist style and in-your-face attitude proved that Harley was again on a roll.

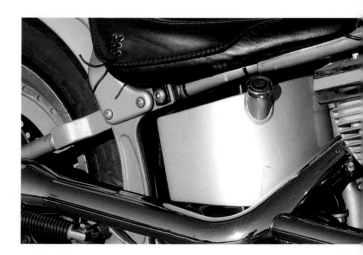

1990 FLSTF specifications

Drivetrain

Engine:	Evolution
Layout:	45-degree V-twin, rigid-mounted
Displacement:	80 cubic inches (1,339 cc)
Cooling:	Air-cooled
Compression ratio:	8.5:1
Fuel system:	40 millimeter Keihin carburetor
Horsepower:	58.0 brake horsepower @ 5,000 rpm
Primary drive:	Chain
Transmission:	Five-speed
Final drive:	Belt

Chassis

Fuel capacity:	4.2 gallon
Wheelbase:	62.5 inches
Weight:	666 pounds (wet)
Seat height (unlade):	26.6 inches

Suspension

Front:	Telescopic forks, 5.1-inch wheel travel
Rear:	Twin shocks, 4.1-inch wheel travel

Brakes

Front:	Single-action caliper, 1 disc
Rear:	Single-action caliper, 1 disc
Wheels:	16 inches (front), 16 inches (rear)

What they said

"I judge motorcycles on how well they go, stop and turn. The Fat Boy doesn't do any of these particularly well, but I guess most buyers don't expect it to. What they expect is a high profile and lots of image, and that the FLST delivers. People love this machine just because it's the newest machine from Milwaukee. They don't care about performance; it's a Harley, and that's what matters." *Motorcyclist*, March 1990 (1990 FLSTF)

"The Fat Boy is happy as the proverbial hog on the interstate, so long as the needle on its pizza-sized speedo stays at or near the national twin-nickel limit."—*Motorcyclist* (1990 FLSTF)

"The rigid-mount engine shakes loose the odd nut or bolt if you don't make the rounds with a wrench every couple of weeks, but hydraulic tappets and electronic ignition keep it from becoming maintenance intensive."—*Motorcyclist* (1990 FLSTF)

Parts prices/cost of typical repairs

Parts and Ownership Costs: Typical H-D dealer labor rate = $90/hour

Maintenance item	Action	Interval*	Estimated cost
Air filter	Inspect, service as required		$12.95
Air suspension	Check pressure, operation, and leakage	Annually	
Base gasket	Inspect as necessary		7.5 hours labor $750 total @ dealer
Battery	Check battery and clean connections. Old flooded-type batteries should be immediately replaced.	Annually	
Brake fluid	Check levels and condition	Check level annually. Flush and replace with new fluid every 2 years	
Brake pads and discs	Inspect for wear	Replace as needed	
Clutch	Check adjustment		
Critical fasteners	Check tightness	Every 5,000 miles	
Cruise control	Inspect disengage switch and components	As required	
Drive belt and sprockets	Inspect, adjust belt	Adjustment should be performed by dealer	
Electrical equipment and switches	Check operation		
Engine oil and filter	Replace	Every 5,000 miles	
Fork oil	Replace	Every 10,000 miles	2.5 hours labor $275 total @ dealer
Fuel door and saddlebags	Lubricate hinges and latches	As required	
Fuel lines and fittings	Inspect for leaks	Annually	
Jiffy stand	Inspect and lubricate	Annually	
Oil lines and system	Inspect for leaks	Annually	
Primary chain case lubricant	Replace	Every 10,000 miles	
Spark plugs	Inspect	Replace every 20,000 miles	
Steering head bearings	Lubricate	50,000 miles	
Throttle, brake, clutch controls	Check, adjust, and lubricate		
Tires	Check pressure, inspect tread		
Transmission lubricant	Replace	Every 20,000 miles	
Wheel spokes	Check tightness		
Wheel bearings			.6 hours labor $120 total @ dealer
Three-fluid change	(Crankcase, primary, transmission oils)		.3 hours labor $170 total @ dealer
20,000 mile service	3 fluid change, all req. maint Check spark plugs		$700 total @ dealer

Note: If the bike has been unused and in storage for more than three years, all of these items should receive immediate attention, and key fluids and lubricants should be drained and replaced.

Usability and collectibility ratings

Usability: ★★ The disc wheels catch cross winds and make the bike harder to handle than other Softails.

Collectibility: ★★★★★ Although later versions don't earn this rating, the original battleship-gray Fat Boy is a true classic.

Recalls and service bulletins

The 1990–1992 Fat Boys were recalled to replace a starter relay that could potentially short circuit. If the relay overheats and the circuit shorts out, it could cause a fire in the relay that could spread to other parts of the motorcycle.

The 1999 Fat Boys were built with a fuel tank vent fitting that could potentially be plugged. This allows the carburetor to overflow fuel and could lead to a fire.

Garage Watch
Key items to look for.

Evo bikes have many common maintenance concerns. A buyer who is seeking an Evo-powered bike should plan to review and prepare to replace the following key items (if the current owner hasn't done so already):
Stator and regulator
Old flooded-type battery
Intake seals
Paper base gaskets (approximately 7.5 hours of labor)
Primary seals

Rigid-mounted Big Twins will definitely send vibrations to the rider through the bars, seat, and floorboards and the Fat One is no exception.

Old flooded-type battery

Starter relay should have been replaced under recall (1990–92).

Stator and regulator

If fuel tank becomes plugged, tank will belch out gas.

Intake seals

Paper base gaskets (approximately 7.5 hours of labor)

Primary seals

69

Chapter 12

1991 to 1998 FXD

Sturgis. Just saying the name of this little town in South Dakota conjures up images of the massive biker rallies held during the first week of every August. The Sturgis rally has been held for 70 years, and a visit to the rally should be on every Harley owner's to-do list. In honor of this event, Harley has used the Sturgis moniker on its bikes several times. Usually, the Sturgis models are special or represent something new from the Motor Company. The 1991 FXDB Sturgis was no exception.

For years, riders enjoyed the long, low FX look. However, there was a growing desire for an updated bike, one that integrated some of Harley's latest technology. Harley engineers responded with an all-new design that would become the Dyna Glide chassis. The chassis was improved in several key areas. The engineers wanted to reduce the amount of engine vibration that was transmitted to the rider. This was a major concern in the old FXR chassis. Vibration was quelled by designing completely new rubber engine mounts. Where the FXR had three rubber engine mounts and twin Heim-joint turnbuckles, the Dyna frame had only two rubber engine mounts and one turnbuckle. The engine and transmission cases were redesigned to bolt directly together, and with the frame and swingarm they form the hidden chassis.

These new cases had oil passages inside (both a functional and cosmetic improvement), a relocated oil filter on the front, and an oil sump enclosed in the transmission case. From a design standpoint, Harley wanted to keep the frame rails narrow and unobtrusive, and it was decreed that the rear shocks would be forward-mounted. The FXR had had rear-mounted shocks that offered better handling characteristics, but they were not as aesthetically pleasing as a forward-mount setup. Form would trump functionality in the new Dyna design, and the rear-mount would be history. The Dyna was a breakthrough for Harley design and engineering. The new chassis was both dynamically rigid and authentic in its styling.

In 1991, the Motor Company introduced the all-new chassis and began to replace the aging FX series. It would underpin the new family of FXD Dyna bikes. The first bike to use the new chassis was the limited-edition 1991 FXDB Sturgis. The FXDB Sturgis was built in limited quantities—only 1,600 were produced for model year 1991. The Sturgis showed just how good the new chassis really was.

There was no doubt that the FXDB was still a "true" Harley. The FXDB's Evo Big Twin sounds just like the FXR's, and the bike is true to the styling roots of the FXR. But the similarities end there. The new chassis and engine mounting system dramatically reduce the amount of vibrations that travel to the rider. At a steady 65 miles per hour, the engine spins at 3,000 rpm and the engine's vibrations are virtually absent. Sure, the vibrations will re-emerge above 3,500 rpm, but there's a sweet spot at 3,000 rpm that allows for comfortable cruising. When the roads get twisty, the new chassis rises to the occasion. The rigid spine of the hidden chassis resists flex far better than the FXR ever could, inspiring confidence and helping the Dyna maintain a steady line through the curves. The new Dyna chassis retained the classic styling but proved to be miles ahead of its predecessor's level of refinement.

Over the next few years, Harley steadily phased out the FXR bikes, replacing them with new models based on the Dyna chassis.

1991 FXDB Sturgis specifications

Drivetrain

Engine:	Evolution
Layout:	45-degree V-twin, rubber-mounted
Displacement:	80 cubic inches (1,339 cc)
Cooling:	Air-cooled
Compression ratio:	8.5:1
Fuel system:	40-millimeter Keihin carburetor
Horsepower:	58.0 brake horsepower @ 5,000 rpm
Primary drive:	Chain
Transmission:	Five-speed
Final drive:	Belt

Chassis

Fuel capacity:	4.9 gallon
Wheelbase:	65.0 inches
Weight:	627 pounds (wet)
Seat height (unlade):	28.5 inches

Suspension

Front:	Telescopic forks, 6.9-inch wheel travel
Rear:	Twin shocks, 3.0-inch wheel travel

Brakes

Front:	Single-action caliper, 1 disc
Rear:	Single-action caliper, 1 disc
Wheels:	19 inches (front), 16 inches (rear)

What they said

"The engine revs willingly to its 5,200 rpm redline, more willingly than any stock Big Twin we've ridden."—*Motorcyclist* (1991 FXDB Sturgis)

"Here's a Harley that appeals to the intellect as well as the emotions. As far as I'm concerned, this is the king of the boulevard." —*Motorcyclist* (1991 FXDB Sturgis)

Most of Harley's efforts, though, went into the new Dyna-Glide frame. It retains the previous FXR-series rectangular backbone layout, but with new castings for the steering head and swing-arm bridge. The centerpiece of the Dyna Glide frame is the new rubber mounts, each a metal block sandwiched between thick rubber pads and steel plates. As before, the mounts isolate the entire driveline—engine, swing arm and rear wheel—but the FXDB uses only two mounts and a single turnbuckle, in place of its predecessor's three less-sophisticated rubber mounts and two turnbuckles. The new system reduces the amount of engine movement, and offers directional stiffness: It's complaint vertically to absorb vibration, and stiff laterally to maintain wheel alignment. Overall, the Dyna Glide frame provides admirable rigidity, yet makes the Sturgis one of the smoothest Harleys ever to come down the pike. —*Cycle*, August 1991

"You'd expect the longest wheelbase in recent history (65.5 inches) would display all the back road agility of a ranch-style split-level. You'd be wrong."—*Motorcyclist* (1992 FXDC Custom)

"Underneath it all is the excellent FXD Dyna Glide chassis, which is a huge step above the old FXR frame."—*Motorcyclist* (1992 FXDC Custom)

Parts prices/cost of typical repairs

Parts and Ownership Costs: Typical H-D dealer labor rate = $90/hour

Maintenance item	Action	Interval*	Estimated cost
Air filter	Inspect, service as required		$12.95
Air suspension	Check pressure, operation, and leakage	Annually	
Base gasket	Inspect as necessary		7.5 hours labor $750 total @ dealer
Battery	Check battery and clean connections. Old flooded-type batteries should be immediately replaced.	Annually	
Brake fluid	Check levels and condition	Check level annually. Flush and replace with new fluid every 2 years	
Brake pads and discs	Inspect for wear	Replace as needed	
Clutch	Check adjustment		
Critical fasteners	Check tightness	Every 5,000 miles	
Cruise control	Inspect disengage switch and components	As required	
Drive belt and sprockets	Inspect, adjust belt	Adjustment should be performed by dealer	
Electrical equipment and switches	Check operation		
Engine oil and filter	Replace	Every 5,000 miles	
Fork oil	Replace	Every 10,000 miles	2.5 hours labor $275 total @ dealer
Fuel door and saddlebags	Lubricate hinges and latches	As required	
Fuel lines and fittings	Inspect for leaks	Annually	
Jiffy stand	Inspect and lubricate	Annually	
Oil lines and system	Inspect for leaks	Annually	
Primary chain case lubricant	Replace	Every 10,000 miles	
Spark plugs	Inspect	Replace every 20,000 miles	
Steering head bearings	Lubricate	50,000 miles	
Throttle, brake, clutch controls	Check, adjust, and lubricate		
Tires	Check pressure, inspect tread		
Transmission lubricant	Replace	Every 20,000 miles	
Wheel spokes	Check tightness		
Wheel bearings			.6 hours labor $120 total @ dealer
Three-fluid change	(Crankcase, primary, transmission oils)		.3 hours labor $170 total @ dealer
20,000 mile service	3 fluid change, all req. maint. Check spark plugs		$700 total @ dealer

Note: If the bike has been unused and in storage for more than three years, all of these items should receive immediate attention, and key fluids and lubricants should be drained and replaced.

Usability and collectibility ratings

Usability: ★★★★ The Dyna frame used a more modern design than found on any previous rubber-mounted Harley.

Collectibility: ★★★ The Dyna bikes are more user-friendly than any previous Harleys, but they've never set Harley fans imaginations on fire.

Recalls and service bulletins

The 1991–1992 FXD models were built with a fuel tank vent that could leak fuel to the ground and cause a fire. Fuel inlet needles were replaced to remedy this condition.
　　The 1991–1992 FXD models were recalled to repair fuel tanks because they leaked when they were impact-tested by H-D, and this could create a fire hazard.

Garage Watch

Key items to look for.

Evo bikes have many common maintenance concerns. A buyer who is seeking an Evo-powered bike should plan to review and prepare to replace the following key items (if the current owner hasn't done so already):

Stator and regulator
Old flooded-type battery
Intake seals
Paper base gaskets (approximately 7.5 hours of labor)
Primary seals

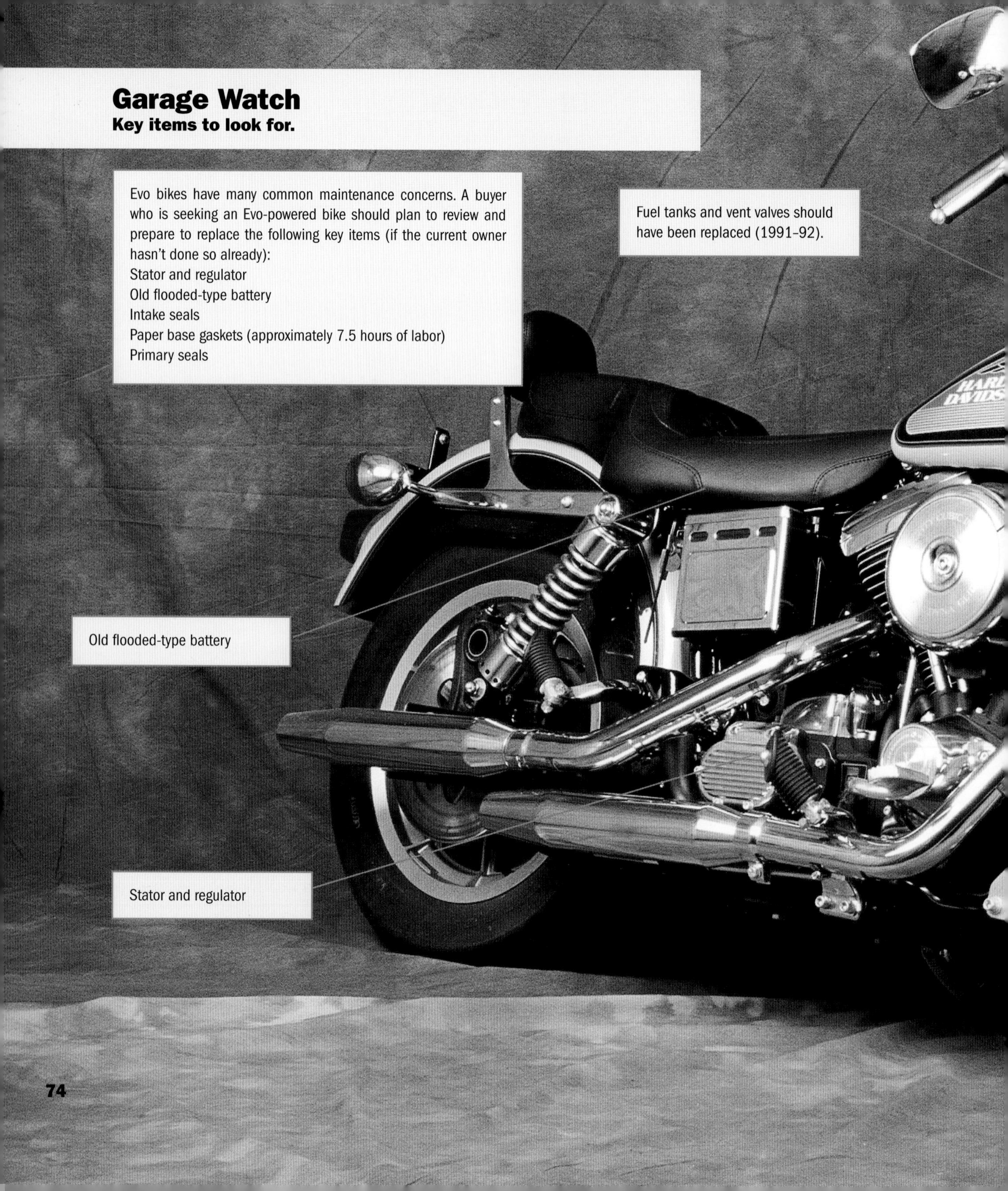
Fuel tanks and vent valves should have been replaced (1991–92).
Old flooded-type battery
Stator and regulator

Intake seals

Paper base gaskets (approximately 7.5 hours of labor)

Primary seals

Chapter 13

1991 to 2003 XL883

When the dust settled after the United States dropped the tariffs on Japanese motorcycles, Harley rose to the occasion. The Motor Company had made major improvements to its model lineup, and Harley could again be taken seriously as a high-quality, competitive motorcycle brand. Of course, the Japanese manufacturers had made serious inroads to the U.S. market with mid-displacement cruisers throughout the 1980s. Honda Shadows and Yamaha Viragos were ubiquitous, and their 750-cc V-twin models were direct competitors to the budget-priced 883-cc Harley Sportster.

As you'll recall, the four-speed Sportster of the 1980s (see chapter 7), was a "traditional" Harley. For 1985, the Sportster was blessed with a version of the Evolution engine, and this transformed the Sportster into a much more modern motorcycle. The Evo alone was not enough to keep the Sportster competitive with Japan, however. The Viragos and Shadows had balanced engines and five-speed—or even six-speed (!)—transmissions. Their seats were more padded, suspensions more plush, and they had full instrumentation. The value proposition of the Japanese bikes was also good, since they were priced close to the MSRP of an XL883. Despite the Evolution engine, this traditional Harley was a tough sell to those who didn't bleed Orange and Black.

For 1991, Sportsters received another set of major powertrain improvements. Finally, the Motor Company was able to build a Sporty with a five-speed. Harley had built Sportsters with four-speed boxes for as long as anyone could remember, and the five-speed was a huge improvement. Adding a fifth ratio was not as simple as it sounds, however. The new transmission required an all-new transmission case, as well as an entirely new set of gears, shafts, bearings, and so on. There was also the addition of a new diaphragm spring clutch, a design derived directly from the clutch of the Big Twin bikes. Oh, and the Motor Company saw fit to add belt drive for the 883 Deluxe model too.

This host of powertrain improvements made the 1991 XL883 the best little Sporty yet built by the Motor Company. The new transmission had revised ratios—shorter in gears 1 to 4, with fifth at a 1:1 ratio. The taller fifth gear greatly improved highway cruising capability. The Sportster's engine was now in a much more relaxed rpm range on the

highway, and fuel economy improved too. The belt final drive of the 883 Deluxe made the driveline notably smoother during shifts and quieter at speed, plus it required much less maintenance than the previous chain drive. Belt final drive would become standard on all Sportsters from model year 1993-on.

The Sportster chassis received many improvements. New rubber-mounted footpegs further isolated the rider from engine vibrations. Self-canceling turn signals were standard, and the new primary case had an inspection cover that made routine maintenance even easier.

Harley engineers had worked hard to improve the littlest Sportster so it could compete with the onslaught of Japanese cruisers. The improved drivetrain made the Sportster far more enjoyable to ride while still maintaining its appeal to the budget-minded Harley purist.

1998 XL883 specifications

Drivetrain

Engine:	Evolution
Layout:	45-degree V-twin, rigid-mounted
Displacement:	54 cubic inches (883 cc)
Cooling:	Air-cooled
Compression ratio:	8.8:1
Fuel system:	40-millimeter Keihin carburetor
Horsepower:	50.0 brake horsepower @ 6,000 rpm
Torque:	49 foot-pounds @ 4,100 rpm
Primary drive:	Chain
Transmission:	Five-speed
Final drive:	Belt

Chassis

Fuel capacity:	3.3 gallons
Wheelbase:	60.0 inches
Weight:	518 pounds (wet)
Seat height (unlade):	27.2 inches

Suspension

Front:	Telescopic forks
Rear:	Twin shocks

Brakes

Front:	four-piston caliper, 1 disc
Rear:	four-piston caliper, 1 disc
Wheels:	21 inches (front), 16 inches (rear)

What they said

"The Sportster's '91 updates are even more extensive than those involved in the switch to the Evolution engine in '85. Where that engine's mods were basically top-end only, this latest Sportster has been revamped from the cases up. The only pieces to escape unchanged are the pistons, con rods, cylinders, and carb. This time, the news revolved around the Sportster's long-awaited five-speed transmission. So much of the engine had to be revised to accept the new gear cluster that H-D took the time to make a few additional improvements, again to bump up quality, simplify assembly, and reduce noise and cost. —*Cycle*, August, 1991

"As satisfying as the redesign was for the Sportster buyer, it turned out to be even more so for The Motor Company, once the sales results were in for that first five-speed year. . . . Sales of the 883 Deluxe more than doubled, to 3,034. Sales of the lower-priced 883 Standard and Hugger were down slightly. . . . Just as had happened earlier with the Big Twin line, Sportster customers were buying more of the upscale models than of the strippers."—Greg Field, *Harley-Davidson Evolution Motorcycles* (1991 Sportsters)

Parts prices/cost of typical repairs

Parts and Ownership Costs: Typical H-D dealer labor rate = $90/hour

Maintenance item	Action	Interval*	Estimated cost
Air filter	Inspect, service as required		$12.95
Air suspension	Check pressure, operation, and leakage	Annually	
Base gasket	Inspect as necessary		7.5 hours labor $750 total @ dealer
Battery	Check battery and clean connections. Old flooded-type batteries should be immediately replaced.	Annually	
Brake fluid	Check levels and condition	Check level annually. Flush and replace with new fluid every 2 years	
Brake pads and discs	Inspect for wear	Replace as needed	
Clutch	Check adjustment		
Critical fasteners	Check tightness	Every 5,000 miles	
Cruise control	Inspect disengage switch and components	As required	
Drive belt and sprockets	Inspect, adjust belt	Adjustment should be performed by dealer	
Electrical equipment and switches	Check operation		
Engine oil and filter	Replace	Every 5,000 miles	
Fork oil	Replace	Every 10,000 miles	2.5 hours labor $275 total @ dealer
Fuel door and saddlebags	Lubricate hinges and latches	As required	
Fuel lines and fittings	Inspect for leaks	Annually	
Jiffy stand	Inspect and lubricate	Annually	
Oil lines and system	Inspect for leaks	Annually	
Primary chain case lubricant	Replace	Every 10,000 miles	
Spark plugs	Inspect	Replace every 20,000 miles	
Steering head bearings	Lubricate	50,000 miles	
Throttle, brake, clutch controls	Check, adjust, and lubricate		
Tires	Check pressure, inspect tread		
Transmission lubricant	Replace	Every 20,000 miles	
Wheel spokes	Check tightness		
Wheel bearings			.6 hours labor $120 total @ dealer
Three-fluid change	(Crankcase, primary, transmission oils)		.3 hours labor $170 total @ dealer
20,000 mile service	3 fluid change, all req. maint Check spark plugs		$700 total @ dealer

Note: If the bike has been unused and in storage for more than three years, all of these items should receive immediate attention, and key fluids and lubricants should be drained and replaced.

Usability and collectibility ratings

Usability: ★★★ The 1991 redesign led to a much more usable motorcycle, but it was still a solid-mounted paint shaker.

Collectibility: ★★ There are two of these for every three garages.

Garage Watch
Key items to look for.

Evo bikes have many common maintenance concerns. A buyer who is seeking an Evo-powered bike should plan to review and prepare to replace the following key items (if the current owner hasn't done so already):
Stator and regulator
Old flooded-type battery
Intake seals
Paper base gaskets (approximately 7.5 hours of labor)
Primary seals

A host of powertrain improvements on the '91 XL883 made the Sportster the "sportiest" H-D to date.

Paper base gaskets (approximately 7.5 hours of labor)

Intake seals

Primary seals

Old flooded-type battery

Stator and regulator

Chapter 14

1991 to 2003 XL1200

The Evolution engine was a major improvement to the 1200 Sportster. When it was first offered in the 1986 bikes, they proved sensational. Their true American style and modernized powerplant set them apart from the prolific UJMs. Sportsters were price-competitive too. But the Evo alone was not enough to keep everyone happy. There remained room to improve the budget models of the Harley lineup.

In 1991, Harley gave the Sportsters' drivelines a major update. The big Evo Sportster had gotten a displacement bump to 1,200 cc in 1988. With that new, larger displacement came revised carburetion and new cams. In 1991, the 1200 got the final drive system that it sorely needed, a five-speed transmission and a belt final drive.

This new final drive required many changes to the chassis. The frame, swingarm, and shocks were relocated to accommodate the belt, and a new belt guard was installed. Of course, the transmission internals are all new, and the primary case was also redesigned. These driveline improvements (and belt final drive) debuted in the 1991 XLH883 and XLH1200.

On the road, the new five-speed made the most of the 1200's powerband. The closer ratios of the five-speed meant that the engine's revs didn't drop so much when shifting, allowing the rider to keep the 1200 in the strongest portion of its powerband. Acceleration improved, and fuel economy improved due to a taller top gear. The engine also operated at a more relaxed rpm when cruising the highway.

Growing demand for the Sportsters required Harley to add a dedicated Sportster engine production line to the Capitol Drive plant. In 1996, the XLH1200 was joined by the 1200S Sport and the 1200C Custom.

The 1200S Sport was true to its namesake, as the bike received some substantial sporting hardware as standard equipment. New brakes were fitted: triple floating discs, lifted from the parts bin of the Bad Boy. The new front suspension consisted of some stout cartridge-type forks that had dual-rate internal springs and were adjustable for spring preload and both compression and rebound damping. The remote piggy-back reservoir rear shocks were also adjustable for preload and damping. Mounted on the rims were sticky Dunlop tires that had more grip. The powertrain was virtually identical to the standard 1200, but these changes to the chassis transformed the handling of the 1200S, making it far more enjoyable to ride on twisty roads.

The 1200C Custom was also true to its namesake. The Sportster Custom received chrome and special trim everywhere. Out front was a 21-inch lace front wheel and out back a slotted disc rear wheel. The low handlebars had "hidden" wiring, and the risers and speedo were bright with chrome. There was even some chrome on the fuel tank's new emblems. The 1200C Custom was long, low, and true to the mission of the Harley factory custom. The Sportster Custom template would expand to include an 883C Custom, which was introduced in 1999.

2001 XL12005 specifications

Drivetrain

Engine:	Evolution
Layout:	45-degree V-twin, rubber-mounted
Displacement:	73 cubic inches (1,199 cc)
Cooling:	Air-cooled
Compression ratio:	8.8:1
Fuel system:	40-millimeter Keihin carburetor
Horsepower:	61.0 brake horsepower @ 5,500 rpm
Torque:	71 foot-pounds @ 3,000 rpm
Primary drive:	Chain
Transmission:	Five-speed
Final drive:	Belt

Chassis

Fuel capacity:	3.3 gallons
Wheelbase:	60.0 inches
Weight:	529 pounds (wet)
Seat height (unlade):	28 inches

Suspension

Front:	Telescopic forks; 6.1-inch travel
Rear:	Twin shocks; 3.1-inch travel

Brakes

Front:	Four-piston caliper, 2 disc
Rear:	Four-piston caliper, 1 disc
Wheels:	19 inches (front), 16 inches (rear)

What they said

"Not since the switch to the Evolution engines has a Harley drivetrain been given so major an update."—*Motorcyclist* (1991 XLH1200 Sportster)

"The '91 Sportster proves that Harley's theme of evolution rather than revolution has once again produced a winner."
—Nick Ienatsch, *Motorcyclist* (1991 XLH1200 Sportster)

Parts prices/cost of typical repairs

Parts and Ownership Costs: Typical H-D dealer labor rate = $90/hour

Maintenance item	Action	Interval*	Estimated cost
Air filter	Inspect, service as required		$12.95
Air suspension	Check pressure, operation, and leakage	Annually	
Base gasket	Inspect as necessary		7.5 hours labor $750 total @ dealer
Battery	Check battery and clean connections. Old flooded-type batteries should be immediately replaced.	Annually	
Brake fluid	Check levels and condition	Check level annually. Flush and replace with new fluid every 2 years	
Brake pads and discs	Inspect for wear	Replace as needed	
Clutch	Check adjustment		
Critical fasteners	Check tightness	Every 5,000 miles	
Cruise control	Inspect disengage switch and components	As required	
Drive belt and sprockets	Inspect, adjust belt	Adjustment should be performed by dealer	
Electrical equipment and switches	Check operation		
Engine oil and filter	Replace	Every 5,000 miles	
Fork oil	Replace	Every 10,000 miles	2.5 hours labor $275 total @ dealer
Fuel door and saddlebags	Lubricate hinges and latches	As required	
Fuel lines and fittings	Inspect for leaks	Annually	
Jiffy stand	Inspect and lubricate	Annually	
Oil lines and system	Inspect for leaks	Annually	
Primary chain case lubricant	Replace	Every 10,000 miles	
Spark plugs	Inspect	Replace every 20,000 miles	
Steering head bearings	Lubricate	50,000 miles	
Throttle, brake, clutch controls	Check, adjust, and lubricate		
Tires	Check pressure, inspect tread		
Transmission lubricant	Replace	Every 20,000 miles	
Wheel spokes	Check tightness		
Wheel bearings			.6 hours labor $120 total @ dealer
Three-fluid change	(Crankcase, primary, transmission oils)		.3 hours labor $170 total @ dealer
20,000 mile service	3 fluid change, all req. maint Check spark plugs		$700 total @ dealer

Note: If the bike has been unused and in storage for more than three years, all of these items should receive immediate attention, and key fluids and lubricants should be drained and replaced.

Usability and collectibility ratings

Usability: ★★★ The 1991 redesign made the 1200 Sportster at least tolerable. A sport edition from the late 1990s had enough improvements to earn four stars.

Collectibility: ★★ These were decent enough motorcycles, but built in such massive quantities that they are fairly common.

Garage Watch
Key items to look for.

Evo bikes have many common maintenance concerns. A buyer who is seeking an Evo-powered bike should plan to review and prepare to replace the following key items (if the current owner hasn't done so already):
Stator and regulator
Old flooded-type battery
Intake seals
Paper base gaskets (approximately 7.5 hours of labor)
Primary seals

Old flooded-type battery

Stator and regulator

Intake seals

Paper base gaskets (approximately 7.5 hours of labor)

Primary seals

Chapter 15

1993-era FLSTN

As the 1990s progressed, Willie G., Louie Netz, and the rest of the design department harvested Motor Company history for styling inspiration. They were recognizing that the Harley buyer was increasingly interested in bikes with classic themes. Baby Boomers were coming into prosperous points of their careers, but they sought motorcycles that evoked a sense of history and classic style. The Heritage Softail Nostalgia is a slice of Harley history, tweaked and colored to appeal to a modern taste.

In its first year (1993), the FLSTN Heritage Softail Nostalgia condensed the historical styling of hardtails and Duo-Glides into an updated package. The Heritage is all about style, and this bike oozes style from every angle. In front of the wide FLH bars is a 16-inch spoke wheel, surrounded by a fat whitewall tire and adorned with a valanced Duo-Glide-style fender. The 1993 Nostalgia earned the nicknames "Cow Glide" and "Moo Glide," mostly due to its furry black-and-white cowhide seat, which accented the black-and-white paint scheme on its fenders and Fat Bob tank. Rounding out the Heritage Nostalgia are medium-sized soft saddlebags and a removable windshield. The saddlebags are fringed leather and large enough to accommodate gear for a weekend trip or a day's commute to work. The stock saddle is adorned with studs and conchos, with a pillion that is comfortable enough for a passenger on a 100-mile day trip.

Underneath the classic styling is the typical Heritage Softail Classic chassis and drivetrain. The front suspension consists of fat Showa telescopic forks, and dual Showa dampers soften the impacts from the Softail rear suspension. The drivetrain is the standard rigid-mounted, 80-cubic-inch Big Twin mated to the five-speed transmission. A fishtail staggered exhaust offers a classic styling touch.

The Heritage Nostalgia is most at home in the city and on quiet country roads. This is a bike for weekend rides, the sunny Saturdays and weekend road trips that take one through the local countryside. At 55 miles per hour in top gear on a country road, the 80-inch mill is turning at a relaxed speed and all is right with the world. The saddle is comfortable, and the windshield and bags offer comfort and capacity that make the Heritage a great weekend trip companion. The Heritage is also a decent commuter bike, as long as your commute doesn't put you on the freeways with an 80-mile-per-hour traffic flow. The comfortable seat and the easy reach to the bars make commuting on the Heritage like rolling a Barcalounger down the highway. And that is certainly something to look forward to after a long day at work.

The Heritage Softail Nostalgia was initially a limited-edition, early-release 1993 model. After the Motor Company quickly sold these initial 2,700 Nostalgia bikes, they wanted to keep the bike in production, so new paint schemes and minor trim changes were made in the following years. After 1993, the model was renamed the Heritage Softail Special instead of Nostalgia. However, the 2700 Moo Glides from 1993 are clearly the most collectible examples of the Heritage Nostalgia.

The Heritage Nostalgia is most at home on the boulevard. It's in its element on Saturday's cruise night or down at the local drive-in. The classic styling touches make it as much fun to ogle as it is to ride, and for many, that's exactly what they want from their Harley.

1994 FLSTN specifications

Drivetrain

Engine:	Evolution
Layout:	45-degree V-twin, rigid-mounted
Displacement:	80 cubic inches (1,340 cc)
Cooling:	Air-cooled
Compression ratio:	9.0:1
Fuel system:	40-millimeter Mikuni CV carburetor with accelerator pump
Horsepower:	58.0 brake horsepower @ 5,000 rpm
Torque:	71.5 foot-pounds @ 2,350 rpm
Primary drive:	Chain
Transmission:	Five-speed
Final drive:	Belt

Chassis

Fuel capacity:	5.2 gallons
Wheelbase:	62.5 inches
Weight:	698 pounds (wet)
Seat height (unlade):	26.5 inches

Suspension

Front:	41-millimeter Showa telescopic forks, 5.1-inch wheel travel
Rear:	Dual Showa shocks, 4.1-inch wheel travel

Brakes

Front:	1 disc
Rear:	1 disc
Wheels:	16 inches (front), 16 inches (rear)

What they said

"From the deeply valanced fenders to the comfortable, hair-still-on Black Angus hide seat . . . to the fishtail-tipped staggered duals, the Special offers enough chrome, lacquer, and eye candy to keep the average motorhead occupied for two to three cups of coffee. This one's as much fun to wash, polish, and generally fawn over as it is to ride."—*Motorcyclist* (1994 FLSTN)

"Motoring south on scenic Pacific Coast Highway aboard the Heritage Softail Nostalgia, I was up to my chinstrap in Hog Heaven. Catching a glimpse of the limited-edition Harley-Davidson in a store-front window, I mention to my riding partner at how attractive the bike is, what with its classic styling, black-and-white paint and cowhide-covered seat and saddlebags. But looks alone won't win my favor. Excessive vibration and too little performance from the 1340cc, pushrod V-Twin sours the ride, as does the lack of cornering clearance afforded by the steel floorboards. And as for the heavy braking, well, I'd need to hit the Nautilus machine more often if I rode this bike all the time."
—*Cycle World*, February 1993 (1993 FLSTN)

"Thirteen grand and change is a lot of money for a motorcycle. But the Heritage Softail Special is more than just a motorcycle. It's therapy."—*Motorcyclist* (1994 FLSTN)

Parts prices/cost of typical repairs

Parts and Ownership Costs: Typical H-D dealer labor rate = $90/hour

Maintenance item	Action	Interval*	Estimated cost
Air filter	Inspect, service as required		$12.95
Air suspension	Check pressure, operation, and leakage	Annually	
Base gasket	Inspect as necessary		7.5 hours labor $750 total @ dealer
Battery	Check battery and clean connections. Old flooded-type batteries should be immediately replaced.	Annually	
Brake fluid	Check levels and condition	Check level annually. Flush and replace with new fluid every 2 years	
Brake pads and discs	Inspect for wear	Replace as needed	
Clutch	Check adjustment		
Critical fasteners	Check tightness	Every 5,000 miles	
Cruise control	Inspect disengage switch and components	As required	
Drive belt and sprockets	Inspect, adjust belt	Adjustment should be performed by dealer	
Electrical equipment and switches	Check operation		
Engine oil and filter	Replace	Every 5,000 miles	
Fork oil	Replace	Every 10,000 miles	2.5 hours labor $275 total @ dealer
Fuel door and saddlebags	Lubricate hinges and latches	As required	
Fuel lines and fittings	Inspect for leaks	Annually	
Jiffy stand	Inspect and lubricate	Annually	
Oil lines and system	Inspect for leaks	Annually	
Primary chain case lubricant	Replace	Every 10,000 miles	
Spark plugs	Inspect	Replace every 20,000 miles	
Steering head bearings	Lubricate	50,000 miles	
Throttle, brake, clutch controls	Check, adjust, and lubricate		
Tires	Check pressure, inspect tread		
Transmission lubricant	Replace	Every 20,000 miles	
Wheel spokes	Check tightness		
Wheel bearings			.6 hours labor $120 total @ dealer
Three-fluid change	(Crankcase, primary, transmission oils)		.3 hours labor $170 total @ dealer
20,000 mile service	3 fluid change, all req. maint Check spark plugs		$700 total @ dealer

Note: If the bike has been unused and in storage for more than three years, all of these items should receive immediate attention, and key fluids and lubricants should be drained and replaced.

Usability and collectibility ratings

Usability: ★★★ Think of this as a Fat Boy without the wind-catching disc wheels.

Collectibility: ★★★★★ There will never be another bike like the original Cow Glide.

Garage Watch
Key items to look for.

Old flooded-type battery

Stator and regulator

92

Evo bikes have many common maintenance concerns. A buyer who is seeking an Evo-powered bike should plan to review and prepare to replace the following key items (if the current owner hasn't done so already):
Stator and regulator
Old flooded-type battery
Intake seals
Paper base gaskets (approximately 7.5 hours of labor)
Primary seals

Intake seals

Paper base gaskets (approximately 7.5 hours of labor)

Primary seals

Chapter 16

1996 to 1999 FLHRI

A new Electra Glide model was added to the family in 1987. The Electra Glide Sport took its styling cues from the FLHTP model that had been sold to police departments for 1986. The Sport had a simple windshield that was less bulky than the bat wing fairings, and it also did not have the large Tour Pak luggage behind the passenger. This stripped-down bagger would ultimately evolve into the Road King. The Sport had been sold to police departments as the FLHTP (with some significant modifications) for years, and it was a proven touring machine. When it was introduced in 1994, the Road King quickly became a runaway success.

The FLHR Road King replaced the FLHS Sport, though it did not stray far from the styling of the FLHS. Out in front, the Road King retains the large removable Plexiglas windscreen, instead of the bat wing fairing of its Electra Glide brethren. Two large hard saddlebags are standard, but the large Tour Pak is not included. The front end uses the "balanced" design of the FLT, yet its large forks closely mirror the appearance of the Hydra Glide forks from the FLH. A notable difference from the FLHS is that the King's big speedometer is located on the tank console. The Road King successfully integrates the best of Harley's touring bike technology into a much more elemental form, all while capturing the classic look of the FLH of the 1960s.

Under the 5-gallon tank is the familiar 80 CI Evo, mated to a five-speed transmission. For 1996, Harley offered an optional electronic fuel injection system, and the benefits of the EFI system were profound. The new Weber system was first seen on the FLTCU, and in 1996 it was offered as an option on all Touring models.

In retrospect, it seems odd that fuel injection was offered as an option rather than just standard equipment. The benefits of electronic fuel injection are many: easier cold starts, easy restarts when hot, smooth idle, a 10 percent increase in torque, and an onboard diagnostic system. The carbureted models appealed to the Harley purists, but a rational buyer would choose the fuel-injected bike without hesitation.

Riding a Road King is a comforting experience. The King has all the components of a true Harley Touring bike, distilled down to the important elements. The big windscreen offers ample protection for the rider, as it channels air far above the rider's head. The screen can also be removed without tools for those slow cruises around town. The saddle is soft and comfortable, yet narrow at the front to make it easier for those with short inseams to reach their feet to the ground. The fuel-injected engine offers excellent throttle response, better fuel economy, and a much smoother power delivery than a carbed engine. The rubber engine mounts do an excellent job of isolating the engine vibes when at speed, though the V-twin can still clearly move around a *lot* when idling. The air-adjustable suspension smoothes out the smaller bumps in the road, but its travel is limited and low-speed chatter can upset the bike's otherwise refined demeanor.

Overall, the Road King is a terrific blend of long-haul comfort and traditional Harley character. Considering that the Road King was a *very* popular model, these models are not likely to be at the top of collectors' wish lists. But the King's classic style, fuel-injection, and excellent road manners make it a very desirable touring bike.

1996 FLHRI Road King specifications

Drivetrain

Engine: Evolution
Layout: 45-degree V-twin
Displacement: 80 cubic inches (1,340 cc)
Cooling: Air-cooled
Compression ratio: 9.2:1
Fuel system: Electronic Sequential Port Fuel Injection (ESPFI)
Horsepower: 61 @ 5,000 rpm
Torque: 75.2 foot-pounds @ 3,000 rpm
Transmission: Five-speed
Final drive: Belt

Chassis

Fuel capacity: 5.0 gallons
Wheelbase: 62.7 inches
Weight: 717 pounds (wet)
Seat height (unlade): 28.2 inches

Suspension

Front: Telescopic fork
Rear: Twin shocks

Brakes

Front: 2 disc, (four-piston caliper)
Rear: 1 disc (four-piston caliper)
Wheels: 17 inches (front), 16 inches (rear)

What they said

"Compared to a carbureted Evo, the injected version is an absolute pleasure to use. No choke required (and none is fitted)—just thumb the starter button, and in half a second, after the starter works its way over the compression hump and finally spins the engine, it roars to life, settling into a nice, smooth idle with instant drive away—no coughing, no backfiring. No problem."—*Motorcycle.com* (1996 FLHRI Road King)

"As first experiences go, there's probably nothing like that first ride. When I climb on the Road King, I get that feeling all over again."
—Jason Black, *Motorcyclist* (1994 Road King)

"Replacing the FLHS Sport, the FLHR Road King was similarly outfitted for minimalist touring: just bags and a windshield."—Greg Field, *Harley-Davidson Evolution Motorcycles* (1994 Road King)

Parts prices/cost of typical repairs

Parts and Ownership Costs: Typical H-D dealer labor rate = $90/hour

Maintenance item	Action	Interval*	Estimated cost
Air filter	Inspect, service as required		$12.95
Air suspension	Check pressure, operation, and leakage	Annually	
Base gasket	Inspect as necessary		7.5 hours labor $750 total @ dealer
Battery	Check battery and clean connections. Old flooded-type batteries should be immediately replaced.	Annually	
Brake fluid	Check levels and condition	Check level annually. Flush and replace with new fluid every 2 years	
Brake pads and discs	Inspect for wear	Replace as needed	
Clutch	Check adjustment		
Critical fasteners	Check tightness	Every 5,000 miles	
Cruise control	Inspect disengage switch and components	As required	
Drive belt and sprockets	Inspect, adjust belt	Adjustment should be performed by dealer	
Electrical equipment and switches	Check operation		
Engine oil and filter	Replace	Every 5,000 miles	
Fork oil	Replace	Every 10,000 miles	2.5 hours labor $275 total @ dealer
Fuel door and saddlebags	Lubricate hinges and latches	As required	
Fuel lines and fittings	Inspect for leaks	Annually	
Jiffy stand	Inspect and lubricate	Annually	
Oil lines and system	Inspect for leaks	Annually	
Primary chain case lubricant	Replace	Every 10,000 miles	
Spark plugs	Inspect	Replace every 20,000 miles	
Steering head bearings	Lubricate	50,000 miles	
Throttle, brake, clutch controls	Check, adjust, and lubricate		
Tires	Check pressure, inspect tread		
Transmission lubricant	Replace	Every 20,000 miles	
Wheel spokes	Check tightness		
Wheel bearings			.6 hours labor $120 total @ dealer
Three-fluid change	(Crankcase, primary, transmission oils)		.3 hours labor $170 total @ dealer
20,000 mile service	3 fluid change, all req. maint Check spark plugs		$700 total @ dealer

Note: If the bike has been unused and in storage for more than three years, all of these items should receive immediate attention, and key fluids and lubricants should be drained and replaced.

Usability and collectibility ratings

Usability: ★★★ The Road King loses a star to its Electra Glide brethren because of its uncomfortable stock seat. It looks good, though.

Collectibility: ★★★★ These bikes were popular from the start and remain so today.

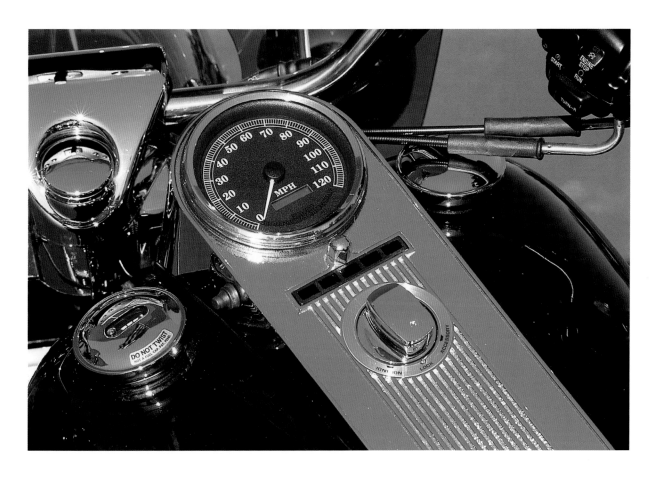

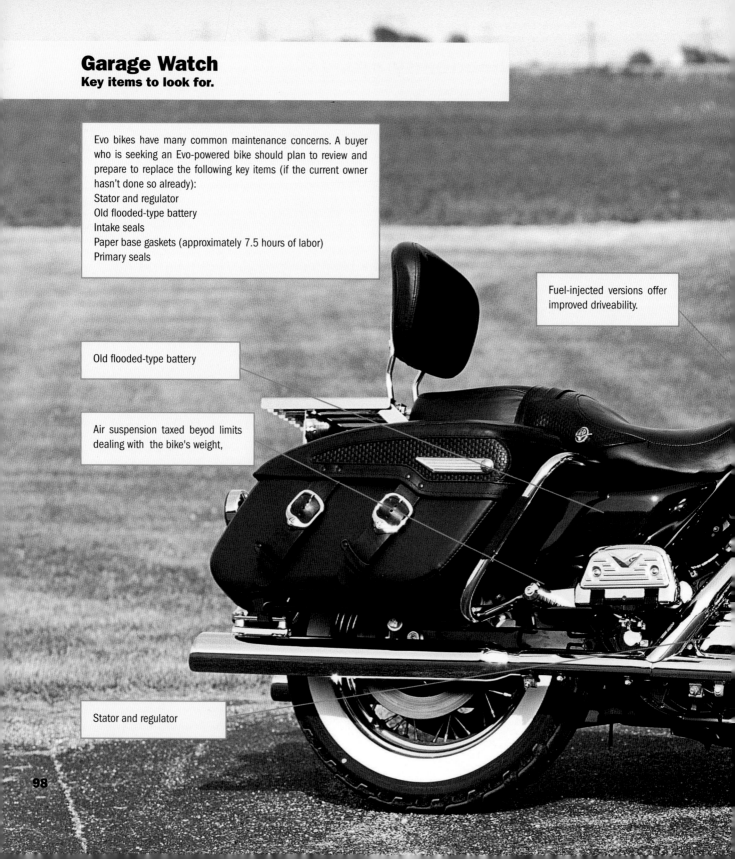

Garage Watch
Key items to look for.

Evo bikes have many common maintenance concerns. A buyer who is seeking an Evo-powered bike should plan to review and prepare to replace the following key items (if the current owner hasn't done so already):
Stator and regulator
Old flooded-type battery
Intake seals
Paper base gaskets (approximately 7.5 hours of labor)
Primary seals

Fuel-injected versions offer improved driveability.

Old flooded-type battery

Air suspension taxed beyod limits dealing with the bike's weight,

Stator and regulator

Intake seals

Primary seals

Paper base gaskets (approximately 7.5 hours of labor)

99

The cult movie *Easy Rider* had a profound effect on the motorcycling scene in America and around the world when it was released in 1969. Almost immediately after the movie hit the big screen that year Harley owners—and owners of other brands of motorcycles, for that matter—began chopping and customizing their bikes. Choppers were the new fad; to mimic Captain America and Billy was to be cool.

As the next decade got underway, even the Harley-Davidson Motor Company realized that it would be cool—not to mention profitable—to offer some models that boasted styling cues similar to those found on the *Easy Rider* bikes. Starting with the original Super Glide, Harley released a string of increasingly wilder custom-styled motorcycles, culminating in the original FXWG Wide Glide, introduced for the 1980 model year. Widely spaced triple trees located the hydraulic fork legs farther apart than on other custom-styled Harley cruisers. Initially, a Shovelhead engine powered the Wide Glide, but in midyear 1984 the new V2 Evolution V-twin replaced the aging cast-iron lump.

The Wide Glide remained in the model lineup until 1986. The iconic Wide Glide returned to the Harley family for 1993, appearing just in time to celebrate the company's 90th anniversary. The new-for-1993 FXDWG Dyna Wide Glide boasted the same masculine and hard-edge appearance that made the original model so popular, but the new edition rolled into dealer showrooms across the nation sporting the now-proven Evo engine and five-speed transmission, even a belt final drive. The five-speed transmission and belt drive, especially, made this *Easy Rider*-inspired bike more easy-riding for its owner when compared to the previous Wide Glide models.

Despite these refinements, the new Wide Glide's overall lines remained pretty much intact for 1993. The widely spaced triple trees still located the hydraulic fork legs, which cradled a 21-inch laced-spoke front wheel sporting an 11.5-inch-diameter brake rotor. The raked triple trees set the FXDWG's overall steering angle at 32 degrees with 5.1 inches of trail, dimensions that project it into the chopper realm.

And that's precisely the styling goal that Harley's design team

intended to reach. The Wide Glide's one-piece Fat Bob gas tank, sculpted seat with passenger bar, bobbed rear fender that partially conceals the taillight, staggered dual shorty mufflers, forward foot controls, small headlight with single-mounting point, and ape-hanger handlebar are styling tricks right out of the custom-chopper playbook. In addition to the limited-edition 90th Anniversary paint scheme, customers could order their Wide Glides with the traditional-style flame paint scheme on the black gas tank, a design treatment Willie G. had introduced on the 1980 model.

The second-generation Wide Glide proved once again that when a bike is styled right, Harley-Davidson's faithful welcome it with open arms and open wallets. And the Wide Glide was certainly styled right—the first time *and* the second time it was offered.

1994 FXDWG Wide Glide specifications

Drivetrain

Engine:	Evolution
Layout:	45-degree V-twin
Displacement:	80 cubic inches (1,340 cc)
Cooling:	Air-cooled
Compression ratio:	8.5:1
Fuel system:	Carbureted
Horsepower:	NA
Torque:	77 foot-pounds @ 3,600 rpm
Primary drive:	Chain, 25/36 ratio
Transmission:	Five-speed
Final drive:	Belt

Chassis

Fuel capacity:	5.2 gallons
Oil capacity:	3.5 quarts
Wheelbase:	66.1 inches
Weight:	598 pounds (wet)
Seat height (unlade):	26.75 inches

Suspension

Front:	Telescopic fork
Rear:	Twin shocks

Brakes

Front:	1 disc
Rear:	1 disc
Wheels:	21 inches (front), 16 inches (rear)

What they said

"The Wide Glide looked good, rode okay and the motor was smooth. No big complaints. The narrow tires seemed to follow the cracks in the road more than the others. The front brake could have been a bit more progressive. Just a good old Harley, like a good old dog, or steady girlfriend."—*Motorcycle Online*

"The Dyna... looks beautiful, it handles with grace, it is the real pushrod twin with the real Big Twin purr, and it is the authentic bodice-ripping bike. It makes beautiful women coo and forget that they don't live at your place. Nuff said."—*Motorcycle Online*

"Not as flashy, bold, or self-consciously nostalgic as the others, but the Wide Glide is still the epitome of cool."
—*Motorcycle Online*

Parts prices/cost of typical repairs

Parts and Ownership Costs: Typical H-D dealer labor rate = $90/hour

Maintenance item	Action	Interval*	Estimated cost
Air filter	Inspect, service as required		$12.95
Air suspension	Check pressure, operation, and leakage	Annually	
Base gasket	Inspect as necessary		7.5 hours labor $750 total @ dealer
Battery	Check battery and clean connections. Old flooded-type batteries should be immediately replaced.	Annually	
Brake fluid	Check levels and condition	Check level annually. Flush and replace with new fluid every 2 years	
Brake pads and discs	Inspect for wear	Replace as needed	
Clutch	Check adjustment		
Critical fasteners	Check tightness	Every 5,000 miles	
Cruise control	Inspect disengage switch and components	As required	
Drive belt and sprockets	Inspect, adjust belt	Adjustment should be performed by dealer	
Electrical equipment and switches	Check operation		
Engine oil and filter	Replace	Every 5,000 miles	
Fork oil	Replace	Every 10,000 miles	2.5 hours labor $275 total @ dealer
Fuel door and saddlebags	Lubricate hinges and latches	As required	
Fuel lines and fittings	Inspect for leaks	Annually	
Jiffy stand	Inspect and lubricate	Annually	
Oil lines and system	Inspect for leaks	Annually	
Primary chain case lubricant	Replace	Every 10,000 miles	
Spark plugs	Inspect	Replace every 20,000 miles	
Steering head bearings	Lubricate	50,000 miles	
Throttle, brake, clutch controls	Check, adjust, and lubricate		
Tires	Check pressure, inspect tread		
Transmission lubricant	Replace	Every 20,000 miles	
Wheel spokes	Check tightness		
Wheel bearings			.6 hours labor $120 total @ dealer
Three-fluid change	(Crankcase, primary, transmission oils)		.3 hours labor $170 total @ dealer
20,000 mile service	3 fluid change, all req. maint Check spark plugs		$700 total @ dealer

Note: If the bike has been unused and in storage for more than three years, all of these items should receive immediate attention, and key fluids and lubricants should be drained and replaced.

Usability and collectibility ratings

Usability: ★★★★ The Dyna frame used a more modern design than found on any previous rubber-mounted Harley.

Collectibility: ★★★ The Dyna bikes are more user friendly than any previous Harleys, but they've never set Harley fans imaginations on fire.

Garage Watch
Key items to look for.

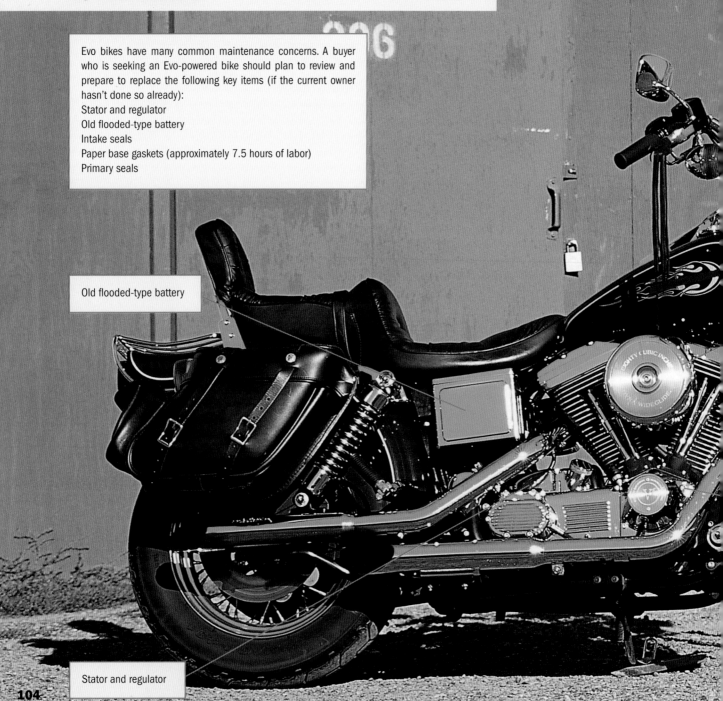

Evo bikes have many common maintenance concerns. A buyer who is seeking an Evo-powered bike should plan to review and prepare to replace the following key items (if the current owner hasn't done so already):
Stator and regulator
Old flooded-type battery
Intake seals
Paper base gaskets (approximately 7.5 hours of labor)
Primary seals

Old flooded-type battery

Stator and regulator

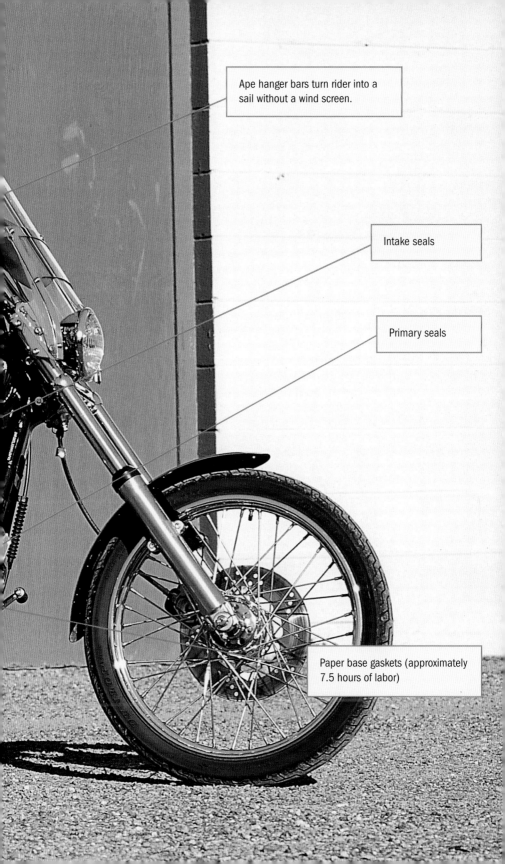

Ape hanger bars turn rider into a sail without a wind screen.

Intake seals

Primary seals

Paper base gaskets (approximately 7.5 hours of labor)

Chapter 18

1996 to 1998 FLHTCUI Electra Glide Ultra Classic and FLTCUI Tour Glide

With much fanfare, Harley-Davidson introduced its new electronic sequential port fuel injection for more precise fuel metering (and lower emissions to help meet clean-air laws that were looming over the horizon) on the 1995 FLHTCUI Electra Glide Ultra Classic. Despite the electronic fuel-management system's leading-edge technology, the new induction was received with a degree of trepidation among the faithful who were used to seeing the familiar single carburetor attached to the right side of their motors. Owners comfortable with lingo that included "main jets," "float bowls," and "choke levers" were confronted with a new language that contained strange words and acronyms like "ECM," "integral throttle body," and "throttle position sensor." The world was changing, even for Harley-Davidson Motor Company.

Despite reluctance by some Harley enthusiasts to embrace electronic fuel injection, the Motor Company forged ahead with the new intake technology, and four models for 1996 were available with the optional induction system. The FLHRI Road King, FLHTCI Electra Glide Classic, and the FLTCUI Tour Glide Ultra Classic joined the FLHTCUI, the "I" at the end of each model designation denoting fuel injection.

Strangely, though, it was Harley's 1996 redesign of the Electra Glide's fairing that created the biggest stir among Harley's devoted customers. The inner fairing dash had been completely reconfigured for a more user-friendly layout. In addition to the new rounded and circular appearance, the one-piece, injection-molded assembly placed the gauges where they were easier to read. Thanks to a precise molding process, the fairing had reinforced ribs molded into the back side for added strength. The new fairing was highlighted with attractive 4-inch speedometer and tachometer gauges in the center and individual 2-inch-diameter analog gauges that contained information about fuel level, oil pressure, voltage, and ambient air temperature. A low-fuel warning light that lit up on the tachometer's face was also integrated into the system.

Harley engineers took the opportunity to simplify the fairing's installation and removal procedures to improve serviceability, reducing mounting hardware from 42 to 14 pieces.

But what really charmed owners to their Ultra Classics were the gizmos and gadgets that came with the bike, starting with electronic cruise control. This was joined by a 20-watt-per-channel, four-speaker AM/FM-cassette stereo system with weather band, separately amplified rear speakers, a remote control for the passenger, and a CB voice-activated intercom with helmet-mounted headsets. Powering this mini-entertainment center was a 445-watt charging system (the carbureted Ultra Classic required only a 360-watt system).

By 1998 electronic fuel injection had proven itself to be reliable and suitable for Harley-Davidson engines. And as America and motorcycle enthusiasts readied themselves for the twenty-first century, Harley-Davidson was gearing up for even more change. A new engine was about to bow, and so 1998 was the final year that the venerable Evolution engine—introduced in 1984—would be used to power an FLH model. The following year Harley-Davidson would introduce the new Twin Cam 88, changing the landscape again for touring enthusiasts who rode bikes built by the Milwaukee-based company.

1996 to 1998 FLHTCUI Electra Glide Ultra Classic specifications

Drivetrain

Engine:	Evolution
Layout:	45-degree V-twin
Displacement:	80 cubic inches (1,340 cc)
Cooling:	Air-cooled
Compression ratio:	8.5:1
Fuel system:	Electronic Sequential Port Fuel Injection
Horsepower:	NA
Torque:	83 foot-pounds @ 3,500 rpm
Primary drive:	Chain, 25/36; 1.44:1
Transmission:	Five-speed
Final drive:	Belt

Chassis

Fuel capacity:	5.0 gallons
Oil capacity:	4 quarts
Wheelbase:	64.7 inches
Weight:	765 pounds (wet)
Seat height (unlade):	28 inches

Suspension

Front:	Telescopic fork
Rear:	Twin shocks

Brakes

Front:	2 disc
Rear:	1 disc
Wheels:	16 inches (front), 16 inches (rear)

What they said

"The FLHTCUI is a bike spawned from years of slow, deliberate improvements. As evidenced by the seven letters in its name, the Ultra Classic is the product of a long, distinguished line of H-D touring motorcycles that are definitely American. Touring in the American idiom simply doesn't get any more American than two 40-inch, air-cooled cylinders splayed 45 degrees apart. Even though two of our Japanese entries are assembled in Nebraska and Ohio, there is something inescapably and essentially American about the primal beat of an 80-inch Milwaukee twin reeling in mile after mile of interstate."—*Motorcycle Online*

"Ergonomics were good, fit and finish were top-notch, and it tied the Wing for range because it's better mileage made up for a 1.3 gallon-smaller tank. Around town it was downright sprightly for its 765 pounds. I felt that, all things considered, it was the best combination of touring and everyday use of this bunch."—*Motorcycle Online*

Parts prices/cost of typical repairs

Parts and Ownership Costs: Typical H-D dealer labor rate = $90/hour

Maintenance item	Action	Interval*	Estimated cost
Air filter	Inspect, service as required		$12.95
Air suspension	Check pressure, operation, and leakage	Annually	
Base gasket	Inspect as necessary		7.5 hours labor $750 total @ dealer
Battery	Check battery and clean connections. Old flooded-type batteries should be immediately replaced.	Annually	
Brake fluid	Check levels and condition	Check level annually. Flush and replace with new fluid every 2 years	
Brake pads and discs	Inspect for wear	Replace as needed	
Clutch	Check adjustment		
Critical fasteners	Check tightness	Every 5,000 miles	
Cruise control	Inspect disengage switch and components	As required	
Drive belt and sprockets	Inspect, adjust belt	Adjustment should be performed by dealer	
Electrical equipment and switches	Check operation		
Engine oil and filter	Replace	Every 5,000 miles	
Fork oil	Replace	Every 10,000 miles	2.5 hours labor $275 total @ dealer
Fuel door and saddlebags	Lubricate hinges and latches	As required	
Fuel lines and fittings	Inspect for leaks	Annually	
Jiffy stand	Inspect and lubricate	Annually	
Oil lines and system	Inspect for leaks	Annually	
Primary chain case lubricant	Replace	Every 10,000 miles	
Spark plugs	Inspect	Replace every 20,000 miles	
Steering head bearings	Lubricate	50,000 miles	
Throttle, brake, clutch controls	Check, adjust, and lubricate		
Tires	Check pressure, inspect tread		
Transmission lubricant	Replace	Every 20,000 miles	
Wheel spokes	Check tightness		
Wheel bearings			.6 hours labor $120 total @ dealer
Three-fluid change	(Crankcase, primary, transmission oils)		.3 hours labor $170 total @ dealer
20,000 mile service	3 fluid change, all req. maint Check spark plugs		$700 total @ dealer

Note: If the bike has been unused and in storage for more than three years, all of these items should receive immediate attention, and key fluids and lubricants should be drained and replaced.

Usability and collectibility ratings

Usability: ★★★★ Fuel injection just made a great touring bike better.

Collectibility: ★★★ These bikes were so popular that there are tens of thousands of them still on the road today.

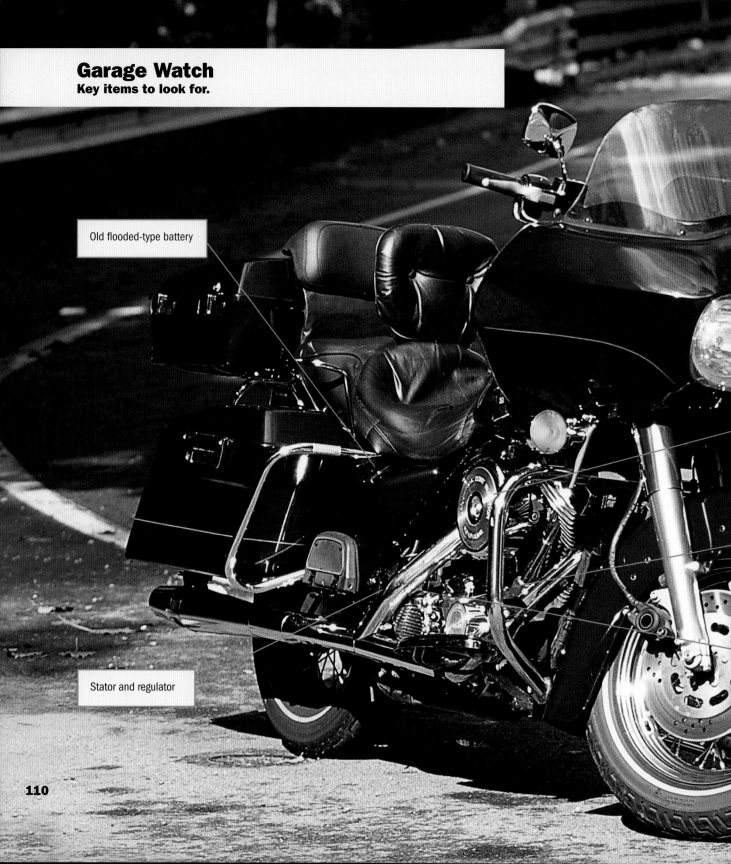

Garage Watch
Key items to look for.

Old flooded-type battery

Stator and regulator

Evo bikes have many common maintenance concerns. A buyer who is seeking an Evo-powered bike should plan to review and prepare to replace the following key items (if the current owner hasn't done so already):
Stator and regulator
Old flooded-type battery
Intake seals
Paper base gaskets (approximately 7.5 hours of labor)
Primary seals

Intake seals

Primary seals

Paper base gaskets (approximately 7.5 hours of labor)

Chapter 19

1997 to 1998 FLSTS Heritage Springer Softail

Heritage has always been a major factor in how Harley-Davidson markets its motorcycles, and it clearly prevailed when the Motor Company introduced its FLSTS Heritage Springer Softail during a special ceremony near San Diego, California, for the 1997 new model. Willie G. Davidson himself was there, and when he introduced the bike to the gathered crowd, he referenced the 1936 Model E as "the grandfather of what we have here on stage."

If the Model E—perhaps better known as the Knucklehead—is the FLSTS's grandfather, then the 1948 Model F—dubbed the Panhead by the faithful—takes its rightful place on the family tree as the Heritage Springer's father. Tom Carson, manager for Harley's product accessories division at the time, said, "I think we really captured the styling of the old bikes with the FLSTS."

Willie G. and Carson were correct in their assessments. The FLSTS carried the nostalgia theme about as far as any new motorcycle ever could, and from stem to stern the bike sporting white paint with red or blue graphics looked the part of a 1948 Panhead. Start at the front where a fender-tip light on the valance fender serves like a shining beacon into Harley's glorious past. And snuggled beneath the springer fork's signature springs sits a chrome-cover horn, mounted exactly the way the Motor Company put them on their bikes more than half a century before. Ditto for the passing lamps on the crossbar beneath the headlight.

Similar retro-theme styling treatments can be found on or near the rear fender. Besides the tombstone-style taillight—originally offered on the Knucklehead before World War II—the Heritage Springer's most notable retro features behind the rider are the tooled black-leather saddlebags with fringe to match the tractor seat. Interestingly, international safety regulations played a role in how long the saddlebag fringe could be. From the beginning, Harley-Davidson intended the Heritage Springer to be an international model for export to other countries, so stylists had to consider foreign vehicle safety codes. One minor hurdle to overcome was Germany's motor vehicle regulations that stipulated maximum length that fringe and other cosmetic trim could be. Steve Piehl, head of Harley's communications

division, said, "We're probably the only motorcycle manufacturer to work with the German safety department for determining the legal length of fringe!" *That's* how important heritage and styling are to the Harley-Davidson Motor Company.

Despite its retro features, the FLSTS boasts the same modern powertrain found on the rest of the 1997 Big Twins. But to help nudge the 80-inch Evo engine into the retro zone, Harley engineers developed old-style crossover exhaust pipes that lead to fishtail mufflers on either side of the 16-inch rear wheel that's wrapped with a wide whitewall Dunlop tire to match that in the front.

Indeed, the nostalgia theme played a huge part in how the FLSTS Heritage Springer Softail came about for 1997. Perhaps Willie G. summed it up best when he said, "Our history is an important part of our future." But as the FLSTS helped prove, Harley-Davidson's future will continue to rely on its past to please its customers.

1997–98 FLSTS specifications

Drivetrain

Engine:	Evolution
Layout:	45-degree V-twin
Displacement:	80 cubic inches (1,340 cc)
Cooling:	Air-cooled
Compression ratio:	8.5:1
Fuel system:	Carbureted
Horsepower:	NA
Torque:	76 foot-pounds @ 3,500 rpm
Primary drive:	Chain, 25/36 1.44:1
Transmission:	Five-speed
Final drive:	Belt

Chassis

Fuel capacity:	4.2 gallons
Oil capacity:	3 quarts
Wheelbase:	63.1 inches
Weight:	690 pounds (dry)
Seat height (unlade):	25.75 inches

Suspension

Front:	Springer fork
Rear:	Twin shocks

Brakes

Front:	1 disc
Rear:	1 disc
Wheels:	16 inches (front), 16 inches (rear)

What they said

"From the digitally cloned horn on the fork to the tombstone-style taillight and fishtail dual exhausts, styling cues borrow heavily from the venerated '48 H-D panhead. The tractor-esque saddle is copiously fringed, as are the embossed leather saddlebags. Harley's latest interpretation of American V-twin chic comes in white, with red or blue striping, plus a suave cloisonné H-D emblem in glorious 3-D—all for a suggested retail price of $17,285."—*Motorcyclist*, September, 1996

Parts prices/cost of typical repairs

Parts and Ownership Costs: Typical H-D dealer labor rate = $90/hour

Maintenance item	Action	Interval*	Estimated cost
Air filter	Inspect, service as required		$12.95
Air suspension	Check pressure, operation, and leakage	Annually	
Base gasket	Inspect as necessary		7.5 hours labor $750 total @ dealer
Battery	Check battery and clean connections. Old flooded-type batteries should be immediately replaced.	Annually	
Brake fluid	Check levels and condition	Check level annually. Flush and replace with new fluid every 2 years	
Brake pads and discs	Inspect for wear	Replace as needed	
Clutch	Check adjustment		
Critical fasteners	Check tightness	Every 5,000 miles	
Cruise control	Inspect disengage switch and components	As required	
Drive belt and sprockets	Inspect, adjust belt	Adjustment should be performed by dealer	
Electrical equipment and switches	Check operation		
Engine oil and filter	Replace	Every 5,000 miles	
Fork oil	Replace	Every 10,000 miles	2.5 hours labor $275 total @ dealer
Fuel door and saddlebags	Lubricate hinges and latches	As required	
Fuel lines and fittings	Inspect for leaks	Annually	
Jiffy stand	Inspect and lubricate	Annually	
Oil lines and system	Inspect for leaks	Annually	
Primary chain case lubricant	Replace	Every 10,000 miles	
Spark plugs	Inspect	Replace every 20,000 miles	
Steering head bearings	Lubricate	50,000 miles	
Throttle, brake, clutch controls	Check, adjust, and lubricate		
Tires	Check pressure, inspect tread		
Transmission lubricant	Replace	Every 20,000 miles	
Wheel spokes	Check tightness		
Wheel bearings			.6 hours labor $120 total @ dealer
Three-fluid change	(Crankcase, primary, transmission oils)		.3 hours labor $170 total @ dealer
20,000 mile service	3 fluid change, all req. maint Check spark plugs		$700 total @ dealer

Note: If the bike has been unused and in storage for more than three years, all of these items should receive immediate attention, and key fluids and lubricants should be drained and replaced.

Usability and collectibility ratings

Usability: ★★★ Low ground clearance meant that it was far too easy to find yourself going too fast in a corner.

Collectibility: ★★★ The bike was unique, but Harley built a pile of them.

Garage Watch
Key items to look for.

Evo bikes have many common maintenance concerns. A buyer who is seeking an Evo-powered bike should plan to review and prepare to replace the following key items (if the current owner hasn't done so already):

Stator and regulator

Old flooded-type battery

Intake seals

Paper base gaskets (approximately 7.5 hours of labor)

Primary seals

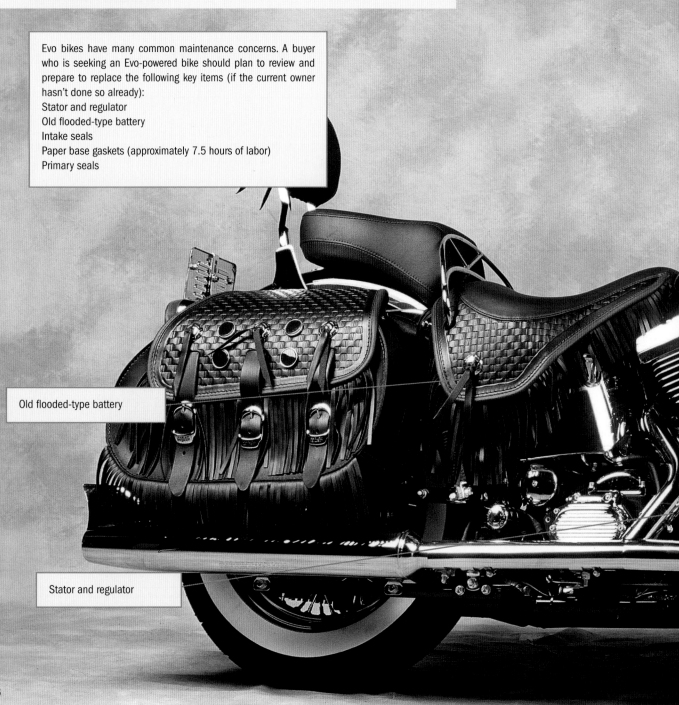

Old flooded-type battery

Stator and regulator

Intake seals

Paper base gaskets (approximately
7.5 hours of labor)

Primary seals

Replace fork bushngs every
10,000 miles.

Chapter 20

1998 FLTR Road Glide

At a glance there's little to distinguish the 1998 FLTR Road Glide from its 1999 successor. Their shark-nose, frame-mounted fairings create similarly distinctive silhouettes, and absence of badges and chrome trim on the front fenders help maintain a clean, uncluttered look. Both models share the same wrinkle-black finish to their engine cases and cylinders, highlighted with polished cylinder fins and chromed primary covers. But if you look closely at their engines, you see the telltale difference between the two model years.

The 1998 FLTR—filling the void created by the demise of the FLTC Tour Glide in 1997—called on the Evolution V2 engine for power. But 1999 happened to be the year that the revolutionary Twin Cam 88 bowed, replacing the single-cam Evo engine that had been Harley's mainstay since 1984. The new, larger-displacement Twin Cam engine offered more power and torque, and as performance tuners were to discover, the TC88's bore centers gave more latitude in how to apply high-performance parts such as big-bore pistons. The Twin Cam 88 also happened to power the 1999 Road Glide and was available with either a carburetor (FLTR) or optional electronic fuel injection (FLTRI), offered only on the 1998 95th Anniversary model that had a two-tone paint job.

In terms of touring amenities, though, both models share many of the same welcomed features. Early FLRT models came with low windshields for an unobstructed view of the road ahead, and the fairings are somewhat aerodynamic too. According to certain magazine road tests of the time, the big fairing helped boost the FLRT's fuel mileage by about 10 percent over the FLHT with its batwing fairing.

The FLRT fairing's dash layout remains uncluttered too. Large-face speedometer and tachometer gauges are centrally located directly beneath the sound system, and on either side and within easy view for the rider sit are the fuel, voltage, oil pressure, and ambient temperature gauges. Two handy—but not lockable—storage compartments are positioned beneath the sound system's two speakers at the fairing's left and right extremities.

The FLTR came with only two lockable saddlebags. Harley stylists wanted to give the FLTR cleaner lines than those of the Electra Glide, and the easiest way to achieve that was to eliminate the bulbous Tour Pak trunk. The visual effects were obvious, and in the words of one magazine road test that helped announce the new 1998 FLTR to enthusiasts: "The bike's sleek lines are uninterrupted, resulting in the cleanest-looking custom to come out of Milwaukee since the Road King."

It was no accident that the Road Glide's appearance is so unique. As Lou Netz, who was vice president of styling at the time, said when the 1998 Road Glide was introduced, "the Motor Company wanted a bike that offered a simplistic, uncluttered" look. And that's exactly what it delivered.

1998 FLTR specifications

Drivetrain
Engine:	Evolution
Layout:	45-degree V-twin
Displacement:	80 cubic inches (1,340 cc)
Cooling:	Air-cooled
Compression ratio:	8.5:1
Fuel system:	Carbureted
Horsepower:	NA
Torque:	76 foot-pounds @ 3,500 rpm
Primary drive:	Chain, 34/46 ratio
Transmission:	Five-speed
Final drive:	Belt

Chassis
Fuel capacity:	5.0 gallons
Oil capacity:	4 quarts
Wheelbase:	63.5 inches
Weight:	762 pounds (wet)
Seat height (unlade):	26.9 inches

Suspension
Front: Telescopic fork	
Rear:	Twin shocks

Brakes
Front:	2 discs
Rear:	1 disc
Wheels:	16 inches (front), 16 inches (rear)

What they said

"H-D's best and least ostentatious touring bike is one of the last heavyweights that still looks and feels like a motorcycle. A big, comfortable motorcycle to be sure, but still a motorcycle. It is one of the few motorcycles in its class that is enjoyable on two lane roads as well as the interstate."—Hogsandparts.com

"Notice the custom influence. It starts with a sleek frame-mounted fairing and low windshield exclusive to this motorcycle. On front in an enclosed twin-oval reflector optic headlight. There is a unique new 'H-D' embossed seat and pillion, which accepts a rider backrest. The overall effect is pure custom touring."—Hogsandparts.com

Parts prices/cost of typical repairs

Parts and Ownership Costs: Typical H-D dealer labor rate = $90/hour

Maintenance item	Action	Interval*	Estimated cost
Air filter	Inspect, service as required		$12.95
Air suspension	Check pressure, operation, and leakage	Annually	
Base gasket	Inspect as necessary		7.5 hours labor $750 total @ dealer
Battery	Check battery and clean connections. Old flooded-type batteries should be immediately replaced.	Annually	
Brake fluid	Check levels and condition	Check level annually. Flush and replace with new fluid every 2 years	
Brake pads and discs	Inspect for wear	Replace as needed	
Clutch	Check adjustment		
Critical fasteners	Check tightness	Every 5,000 miles	
Cruise control	Inspect disengage switch and components	As required	
Drive belt and sprockets	Inspect, adjust belt	Adjustment should be performed by dealer	
Electrical equipment and switches	Check operation		
Engine oil and filter	Replace	Every 5,000 miles	
Fork oil	Replace	Every 10,000 miles	2.5 hours labor $275 total @ dealer
Fuel door and saddlebags	Lubricate hinges and latches	As required	
Fuel lines and fittings	Inspect for leaks	Annually	
Jiffy stand	Inspect and lubricate	Annually	
Oil lines and system	Inspect for leaks	Annually	
Primary chain case lubricant	Replace	Every 10,000 miles	
Spark plugs	Inspect	Replace every 20,000 miles	
Steering head bearings	Lubricate	50,000 miles	
Throttle, brake, clutch controls	Check, adjust, and lubricate		
Tires	Check pressure, inspect tread		
Transmission lubricant	Replace	Every 20,000 miles	
Wheel spokes	Check tightness		
Wheel bearings			.6 hours labor $120 total @ dealer
Three-fluid change	(Crankcase, primary, transmission oils)		.3 hours labor $170 total @ dealer
20,000 mile service	3 fluid change, all req. maint Check spark plugs		$700 total @ dealer

Note: If the bike has been unused and in storage for more than three years, all of these items should receive immediate attention, and key fluids and lubricants should be drained and replaced.

Usability and collectibility ratings

Usability: ★★★★ The Road Glide's cut-down frame-mounted fairing works even better than the full-sized unit of the original FLT.

Collectibility: ★★★★ The Road Glide was as cool as the original FLT was dorky.

Garage Watch
Key items to look for.

Evo bikes have many common maintenance concerns. A buyer who is seeking an Evo-powered bike should plan to review and prepare to replace the following key items (if the current owner hasn't done so already):
Stator and regulator
Old flooded-type battery
Intake seals
Paper base gaskets (approximately 7.5 hours of labor)
Primary seals

Fairing storage compartments non-lockable

Old flooded-type battery

Optional fuel injection improved driveablity.

Stator and regulator

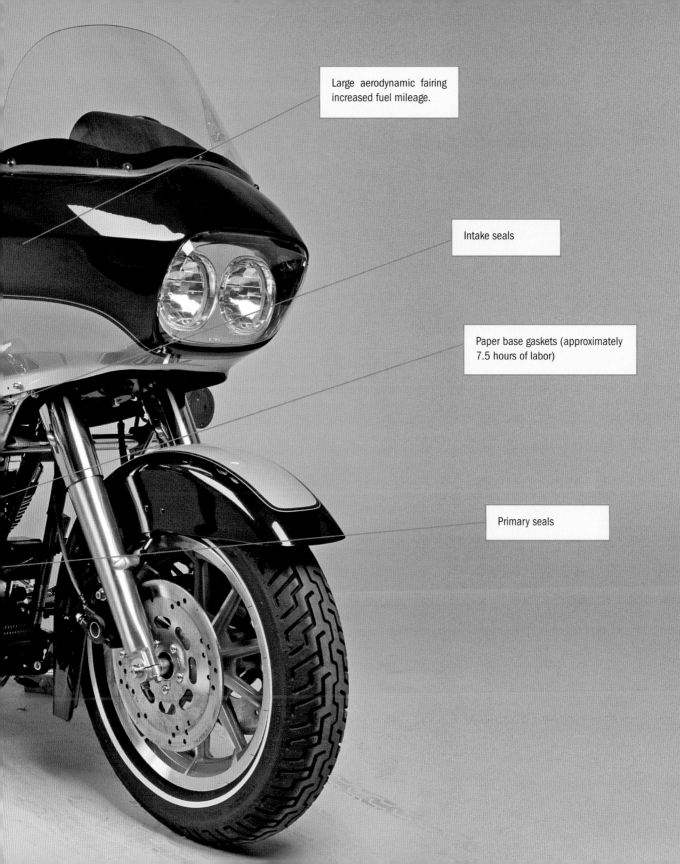

Large aerodynamic fairing increased fuel mileage.

Intake seals

Paper base gaskets (approximately 7.5 hours of labor)

Primary seals

123

Chapter 21
1999 to 2006 FXD Dyna Glides

The FXD Dyna Super Glide is considered the "basic" motorcycle in Harley-Davidson's Big Twin lineup. The FXD comes with few, if any, frills or options, and its MSRP is the lowest of all the Big Twin models. What you get for your money is a motorcycle without a fairing, saddlebags, windshield, or even a tachometer. You know, a basic motorcycle.

But it hasn't always been that way for the Super Glide. Indeed, the Super Glide name has a storied and interesting past. The nameplate arrived in 1971 when Willie G. Davidson convinced Harley-Davidson management to think—and step—outside the box to create what amounted to the first "factory custom," that being the FX Super Glide.

Willie G.'s FX formula was simple: Strip down the frame of an FLH touring model, attach to it the slender, lightweight fork from an XL Sportster, give the package new and refreshing sheet metal and seat, and splash on exciting and racy paint graphics. It's been a successful formula ever since, and the Super Glide has served as the styling canvas for all other Dyna-based models to come. As Willie G. once stated: "The 1971 FX was the seed for the entire FX lineup that today comprises a major portion of our overall volume."

That, of course, means that all improvements and refinements for Dyna models starts with the Super Glide. And for 1999 that meant replacing the 80-cubic-inch Evolution engine with the new Twin Cam 88. Optional onboard security systems were available for all Big Twins, the Super Glide included, in 2001. The same transmission shifting mechanism used in the Twin Cam 88B engine was slipped into the Dyna's gearbox too, offering smoother shifting and a more positive feel when selecting neutral. The electrical fuse box was also given better access for easier servicing.

In keeping up with the times—that is to say fatter rear tires on motorcycles—Harley slipped a 150mm-wide rear tire on the Dyna for 2002. A subtle styling change for that year included the bullet-shape turn signals and repositioned rear footpegs for more passenger comfort. The following year—Harley's 100th anniversary celebration—included anniversary graphics, although the Super Glide's engine cases retained their natural finish, a styling feature that helps identify the FXD.

Electronic fuel injection became an option for the Dyna line in 2004, as denoted by the "I" at the end of the particular model's identification. Thus, the fuel-injected Super Glide was known as the FXDI. Redesigned clutch springs helped minimize effort at the clutch lever, and the gas tank for 2004 was stretched ever so slightly for a more modern look.

A new clear-lens headlight with reflector optics highlighted the 2005 model, but the really big news came in 2006 with the new Cruise Drive six-speed transmission. Only the Dyna models received the six-speed gearbox for 2006; not until 2007 would the rest of the Big Twin lineup receive the new transmission along with the Twin Cam 96 engine. But just to make sure the Twin Cam 88 for 2005 remained up to the challenge of logging countless miles in a day, the engine received a new hydraulic cam-chain tensioner and an improved oil pump for 10 percent more flow and 23 percent more scavenging.

1999 to 2006 Dyna specifications

Drivetrain

Engine:	Twin Cam 88
Layout:	45-degree V-twin
Displacement:	88 cubic inches (1,450 cc)
Cooling:	Air-cooled
Compression ratio:	8.8:1
Fuel system:	Carbureted
Horsepower:	NA
Torque:	82 foot-pounds @ 3,500 rpm
Primary drive:	Chain, 25/36 1.44:1
Transmission:	Five-speed
Final drive:	Belt

Chassis

Fuel capacity:	4.9 gallons
Oil capacity:	3 quarts
Wheelbase:	65.5 inches
Weight:	614 pounds (dry)
Seat height (unlade):	26.5 inches

Suspension

Front:	Telescopic fork
Rear:	Twin shocks

Brakes

Front:	2 disc
Rear:	1 disc
Wheels:	19 inches (front), 16 inches (rear)

What they said

"The Twin Cam 88 is an into-the-parking-lot home fun. It doesn't leak, it doesn't break, and it doesn't take a back seat to any of the imitation big twins from Japan. The fact that it's Harley's best chassis since the FXRS-Sp doesn't hurt matters, either." —*Motorcyclist*, November, 1998

"This Hog revs a little when you twist the throttle and shoots out of corners almost sportily, even if the riding position makes whoever's riding it feel like they're being swallowed butt first by a giant clam."—*Motorcyclist*, November, 1998

"The Dyna Super Glide Sport is far and away the most ridable and most grin-producing Harley-Davidson I've ever ridden." —*Motorcyclist*, November, 1998

Parts prices/cost of typical repairs

Parts and Ownership Costs: Typical H-D dealer labor rate = $90/hour

Maintenance item	Action	Interval*	Estimated cost
Air filter	Inspect, service as required		$12.95
Air suspension	Check pressure, operation, and leakage	Annually	
Base gasket	Inspect as necessary		7.5 hours labor $750 total @ dealer
Battery	Check battery and clean connections. Old flooded-type batteries should be immediately replaced.	Annually	
Brake fluid	Check levels and condition	Check level annually. Flush and replace with new fluid every 2 years	
Brake pads and discs	Inspect for wear	Replace as needed	
Clutch	Check adjustment		
Critical fasteners	Check tightness	Every 5,000 miles	
Cruise control	Inspect disengage switch and components	As required	
Drive belt and sprockets	Inspect, adjust belt	Adjustment should be performed by dealer	
Electrical equipment and switches	Check operation		
Engine oil and filter	Replace	Every 5,000 miles	
Fork oil	Replace	Every 10,000 miles	2.5 hours labor $275 total @ dealer
Fuel door and saddlebags	Lubricate hinges and latches	As required	
Fuel lines and fittings	Inspect for leaks	Annually	
Jiffy stand	Inspect and lubricate	Annually	
Oil lines and system	Inspect for leaks	Annually	
Primary chain case lubricant	Replace	Every 10,000 miles	
Spark plugs	Inspect	Replace every 20,000 miles	
Steering head bearings	Lubricate	50,000 miles	
Throttle, brake, clutch controls	Check, adjust, and lubricate		
Tires	Check pressure, inspect tread		
Transmission lubricant	Replace	Every 20,000 miles	
Wheel spokes	Check tightness		
Wheel bearings			.6 hours labor $120 total @ dealer
Three-fluid change	(Crankcase, primary, transmission oils)		.3 hours labor $170 total @ dealer
20,000 mile service	3 fluid change, all req. maint Check spark plugs		$700 total @ dealer

Note: If the bike has been unused and in storage for more than three years, all of these items should receive immediate attention, and key fluids and lubricants should be drained and replaced.

Usability and collectibility ratings

Usability: ★★★★ The addition of the Twin-Cam engine made the Dyna bikes much less agrarian.

Collectibility: ★★ Even with an all-new engine, the Dyna family is still the red-headed step child of Harley Big Twins.

Garage Watch
Key items to look for.

Early Twin Cams suffered almost universal catastrophic cam-bearing failures. This problem should have been solved in all bikes still on the road, but make sure.

Redesigned clutch springs

Improved oil pump

Photo by David Blattel

On 2006 FXDWGI models check the hole in the handlbars where the wires exit between the handlebar clamps for cracks. A recall at that time saw many of these handlebars replaced.

Optional fuel injection (2004–on)

Improved fork sliders

6-speed transmission in 2006

Chapter 22

2000 to 2007 Softail

When the Softail lineup was overhauled for model year 2000, the Deuce was the eye candy of the family. Its curvy shapes and custom details made it the center of attention at any gathering.

The Deuce was the factory custom that rolled off the line of Harley-Davidson's York Assembly Plant. The design pulls elements of contemporary customs and 1970s choppers together into a modern bike. In a nutshell, the Deuce looks good and performs well too!

Chrome and custom styling touches are everywhere on the Deuce. The long, raked front end is covered in chrome, and it rolls on a brightly chromed 21-inch wire-spoked wheel. All the key front-end components are chromed—the triples, the curved handlebar risers, fork sliders, headlight nacelle, and mirrors—only the fender and brake were spared from the chrome treatment. The swept handlebars are low and wide, framing the 4.9-gallon fuel tank. Mounted on the top of the tank is a long, chromed console that houses the Deuce's speedometer and ignition switch. But chrome is the recurring theme on the Deuce. There's plenty of it throughout the rest of the bike. The horseshoe-shaped oil tank is covered in chrome, wrapping around the frame beneath the rider's seat. The over-under dual exhaust is chromed, as is the rear fender trim, engine and transmission cases, and, well, you get the picture.

The Deuce is not only a good-looking bike, it is entertaining to ride. The Twin Cam 88B powers it, producing 63 horsepower and a broad torque curve. The 88B is solid-mounted to the Deuce's frame, and as its "B" moniker suggests, it is counterbalanced to greatly reduce vibration levels that are transmitted to the rider. The 88B is backed up by the familiar five-speed transmission and belt final drive. This drivetrain is ideally suited to the Deuce's mission as a boulevard cruiser, and it has surprisingly good fuel economy to boot.

On the highway, the Deuce can cruise comfortably at freeway speeds. There are no bags, fairings, or bodywork, so it rarely feels underpowered. Cornering clearance is surprisingly good for a bike with such a radically raked front end (34 degrees!) and long wheelbase. When the corners are smooth, the Deuce is a confident partner on curvy roads. Around town, the Deuce is truly in its element as a stylish boulevard cruiser. The seating position is typical for a cruiser with forward hand and foot controls. The hidden Softail rear suspension is tuned for comfort, and it is at its best when the bike is ridden at around-town speeds. This arrangement clearly works nicely for short hauls and around town, though one's butt may get tired on a long highway jaunt.

As good as the Deuce's performance is, this bike is really all about style. From its chrome-laden front end to the tips of its shotgun exhaust, the Deuce is the epitome of Harley's custom style for this decade. Buyers of a Softail Deuce will be rewarded with a bike that looks great and performs admirably well.

2007 FLSTF Fat Boy specifications

Drivetrain

Engine:	Twin Cam 96B
Layout:	45-degree V-twin, rigid-mounted
Displacement:	96 cubic inches (1,584 cc)
Cooling:	Air-cooled
Compression ratio:	9.2:1
Fuel system:	ESPFI (Electronic Sequential Port Fuel Injection)
Horsepower:	68.0 brake horsepower @ 5,200 rpm
Torque:	90 foot-pounds @ 3,000 rpm
Primary drive:	Chain
Transmission:	Six-speed
Final drive:	Belt

Chassis

Fuel capacity:	5.0 gallons
Wheelbase:	64.5 inches
Weight:	714 pounds (wet)
Seat height (unlade):	27.5 inches

Suspension

Front:	Telescopic forks
Rear:	Twin shocks

Brakes

Front:	1 disc
Rear:	1 disc
Wheels:	17 inches (front), 17 inches (rear)

What they said

"Judging from the comments our sample bike elicited, the Deuce is the best-looking full production motorcycle gracing any showroom."—*Motorcycle Cruiser* (2000 FXSTD Deuce)

"Power delivery is creamy, with a good helping of that torquey low-rev rumble for which Big Twins are famous. The true beauty of the counter-balanced engine is its silky-smooth running at freeway speeds. As we left the desert floor and climbed into the mountains, the Deuce took to the sweeping 70-mph curves with ease. Bending the bike into corners requires only a light touch on the low-rise, flat-track-style bar, although quick side-to-side transitions are a bit of work."—*Cycle World*, February

"You would be hard-pressed to fine a more refined cruiser ride than the 2007 Fat Boy, a bike I've begun referring to as the Sultan of Smooth. It starts without fuss, 'carburates' cleanly, leaks nary a drop of lubricant, settles easily into its sixth-gear lope and generally behaves as though it should be named Choir Boy."—*Cycle World*, January 2007

Parts and Ownership Costs

1,000-mile service: Includes all drivetrain fluid changes and 30-point inspection and adjustments, $275 to $350 (at a Harley-Davidson dealer). Total parts costs are typically around $100.

Twin Cam 96: Key fluid change intervals.

Engine oil and filter: 1,000-mile service, every 5,000 miles thereafter.

Engine primary chaincase drain: -1,000-mile service, 10,000 miles, then every 10,000 miles thereafter.

Cruise drive transmission drain: 1,000 miles, every 20,000 miles thereafter.

Usability and collectibility ratings

Usability: ★★★ It may have a counterbalanced engine, but it still has disc wheels.

Collectibility: Too early to determine.

Garage Watch

Key items to look for.

Early Twin Cams suffered almost universal catastrophic cam-bearing failures. This problem should have been solved in all bikes still on the road, but make sure.

Rear disc wheels on Deuce models catches crosswinds.

Counterbalanced "B" engine smoothest Harley yet

Optional fuel injection improves driveability

Older 5-speed gearbox not as refined as newer 6-speed

Brakes better, but still weak

135

Chapter 23

1999 to 2007 FLH/FLTR

The frame-mounted fairing sets the FLTR apart from the rest of Harley's Touring family, both stylistically and functionally. The "shark-nose" look is undoubtedly different from the rest of the Touring bikes. When parked alongside a Road King or an Electra Glide, the FLTR Road Glide's high, pointy nose creates a very different profile. Regardless of one's opinion of the style, the Road Glide's broad fairing offers excellent wind protection, diverting the wind blast over the rider's head. The fairing also has ample room for comprehensive cockpit-style instrumentation and a powerful stereo. The frame-mounted fairing also has performance advantages. Since the steering head is independent of the fairing, the Road Glide's steering feels notably lighter in slow-speed riding situations. The bike's highway stability is also good, since wind gusts do not get transmitted to the steering.

The Touring bikes (including the Road Glide) received a series of important performance upgrades during the early 2000s. These upgrades were aimed at improving the bikes' highway stability and cornering behavior.

This FL chassis dates back to 1980, when the FLTR was first introduced. As more engine power and weight-carrying capacity increased, the FL chassis began to buckle under the stress. Riders frequently complained about the FL chassis' instability at high speeds (70 miles per hour and up) and in certain cornering situations. There are a few distinct reasons that this was occurring. By design, the FLTR's engine and swingarm are bolted solidly together, and this subassembly is then installed into the chassis and supported with rubber mounts. The rubber mounts do a good job of isolating vibration, but the design prohibits the engine from acting as a "stressed" member of the chassis. Long after its initial development, this old FL chassis was also adapted to accommodate a belt final drive, replacing the former chain drive. To create room for the drive belt system, the rear wheel was actually offset from the front wheel, positioning it out of the same linear plane as the front.

The result was a chassis pushed to its limits. Riders of FL bikes frequently commented on the bike's feel of being "hinged" in the middle, flexing substantially when under cornering loads and oscillating at high speeds or in crosswinds. The Motor Company worked to remedy this, and model year 2002 models received stout new swingarms, new engine mounts, and revised suspension tuning.

The FLTR's key design features and styling changed little during model years 2001–2007. There are clearly variations in minor trim and color options, but the core of the bike remained relatively unchanged during this period. A key item for a buyer's consideration is fuel injection. This was a low-cost option on FLTRs, but it is a desirable feature on a used bike.

Given a choice between an FLTR from this era and a newer model with the new Touring chassis, we clearly recommend a newer model (model year 2009 and up). The new Touring chassis has dramatically improved the handling performance and overall stability of the Touring bikes. Despite the ubiquity of Touring models in the used market from this 2001–2007 era, we would strongly recommend spending some additional money and choosing a model that is from model year 2009 or newer.

2005 FLTRI specifications

Drivetrain

Engine: Twin cam 88
Layout: 45-degree V-twin
Displacement: 88 cubic inches (1,449 cc)
Cooling: Air-cooled
Compression ratio: 8.9:1
Fuel system: Electronic Sequential Port Fuel Injection (ESPFI)
Horsepower: 67 @ 5,200 rpm
Torque: 80.4 foot-pounds @ 3,400 rpm
Transmission: Five-speed
Final drive: Belt

Chassis

Fuel capacity: 5 gallons
Wheelbase: 63.5 inches
Weight: 762 pounds (dry)
Seat height (unlade):   26.9 inches

Suspension

Front: Telescopic fork
Rear: Twin shocks, air-adjustable

Brakes

Front: 2 disc, (four-piston caliper)
Rear: 1 disc (four-piston caliper)

What they said

"The riding position suited my five-foot-ten frame quite well, and the handlebar bend was comfortable. The rubber mounts for the 1450cc V-Twin thoroughly snuff vibration. In terms of comfort, my only possible complaint was the saddle, which seems softer than the Road King's and bottoms out too quickly on all-day rides."—*Motorcycle Cruiser* (2003 FLTRI Road Glide)

"Vertically challenged riders appreciate sitting about 2 inches lower than on most other FL models. The stock 4.5-inch wind deflector is okay if you're under 5-foot-10m but tall riders will want something closer to an actual windscreen, along with more legroom. Still, the coolest 'Glide is a bona fide transcontinental ride, with a pair of lockable hard bags capable of taking on a reasonable amount of road-trip essentials and decent range. The 5-gallon tank is good for an easy 170-190 miles between gas stops, depending on how much weight you're carrying and how fast."—*Motorcyclist*

Parts prices/cost of typical repairs

Parts and Ownership Costs: Typical H-D dealer labor rate = $90/hour

Maintenance item	Action	Interval*	Estimated cost
Air filter	Inspect, service as required		$12.95
Air suspension	Check pressure, operation, and leakage	Annually	
Base gasket	Inspect as necessary		7.5 hours labor $750 total @ dealer
Battery	Check battery and clean connections. Old flooded-type batteries should be immediately replaced.	Annually	
Brake fluid	Check levels and condition	Check level annually. Flush and replace with new fluid every 2 years	
Brake pads and discs	Inspect for wear	Replace as needed	
Clutch	Check adjustment		
Critical fasteners	Check tightness	Every 5,000 miles	
Cruise control	Inspect disengage switch and components	As required	
Drive belt and sprockets	Inspect, adjust belt	Adjustment should be performed by dealer	
Electrical equipment and switches	Check operation		
Engine oil and filter	Replace	Every 5,000 miles	
Fork oil	Replace	Every 10,000 miles	2.5 hours labor $275 total @ dealer
Fuel door and saddlebags	Lubricate hinges and latches	As required	
Fuel lines and fittings	Inspect for leaks	Annually	
Jiffy stand	Inspect and lubricate	Annually	
Oil lines and system	Inspect for leaks	Annually	
Primary chain case lubricant	Replace	Every 10,000 miles	
Spark plugs	Inspect	Replace every 20,000 miles	
Steering head bearings	Lubricate	50,000 miles	
Throttle, brake, clutch controls	Check, adjust, and lubricate		
Tires	Check pressure, inspect tread		
Transmission lubricant	Replace	Every 20,000 miles	
Wheel spokes	Check tightness		
Wheel bearings			.6 hours labor $120 total @ dealer
Three-fluid change	(Crankcase, primary, transmission oils)		.3 hours labor $170 total @ dealer
20,000 mile service	3 fluid change, all req. maint Check spark plugs		$700 total @ dealer

Note: If the bike has been unused and in storage for more than three years, all of these items should receive immediate attention, and key fluids and lubricants should be drained and replaced.

Usability and collectibility ratings

Usability: ★★★★ Twin Cam Harley touring bikes are about as practical as Japanese sedans (but much cooler). This one loses a few points because of its cut-down seat and shortened suspension.

Collectibility: ★★★★ The original frame-mounted fairing wasn't a hit with the faithful, but the cool, stripped-down version on the Road Glide is extremely popular.

Garage Watch
Key items to look for.

Early Twin Cams suffered almost universal catastrophic cam-bearing failures. This problem should have been solved in all bikes still on the road, but make sure.

A low-cost option on the FLTRs was fuel injection and is desirable when looking at a used bike.

2002 and onward FLs featured significant changes to the chassis that improved handling considerably.

Old-tech chassis not stable at speed or in crosswinds.

Stator and regulator

Heat buildup in cockpit area

Brakes better but still weak

Chapter 24
2002–onward
VRSCA/AW/B/F/R/X

For model year 2002, Harley finally introduced its long-rumored liquid-cooled V-twin engine. The V-Rod (VRSCA) was a major departure from the traditional Harley recipe. Powered by a liquid-cooled 1,131-cc DOHC V-twin dubbed the "Revolution," the V-Rod was far more powerful than any other bike in the Motor Company's lineup. This potent new engine was designed with help from Porsche, mated to a transmission designed by Getrag, and installed into an all-new power cruiser chassis that was long and low.

The V-Rod (VRSCA) was the first model of this controversial new family of Harley "performance custom motorcycles." Dressed entirely in silver, with solid disc wheels front and rear, the V-Rod was dramatic and different. The liquid-cooled Revolution engine produced 115 horsepower at 8,250 rpm in its first iteration and had a redline of 9,000 rpm. This is roughly twice the horsepower of a contemporary Twin Cam 88 and a much higher redline than any Harley air-cooled mill. To call the V-Rod different from other Harleys would be a gross understatement.

The motorcycle press raved about the new V-Rod and its Revolution engine. "The V-Rod is like nothing we ever expected Harley to produce, but we're sure glad they did," gushed Motorcycle.com. "Yep, the Motor Company finally did a cutting-edge motor, and they did it right," said the riders at *Motorcycle Daily*.

Over the next few years, new variants of the V-Rod appeared. The VRSCB, Night Rod, Street Rod, V-Rod Muscle, and the VRSCX offered unique interpretations of the liquid-cooled cruiser. For those who want a true factory-built race bike, Harley even offered the VRXSE Destroyer, which is a drag strip-only bike that is capable of sub–10-second quarter-miles.

The VRSCR Street Rod was offered for a short two-year run, from 2006 to 2007. The Street Rod was quite different from the other Revolution-powered bikes. The "R" stands for Roadster, indicating that it's a more sporting version of the VRSC. Its suspension has extended travel, so it can better absorb large bumps and is not as stiff as other V-Rod models. The seating position rotates riders forward and mid-mount controls allow riders to put their weight on the pegs. The result is the most sporting of the V-Rods, a bike that can.

In 2007, the VRSCAW was introduced. It was the successor to the original V-Rod (VRSCA), but it incorporated some significant chassis design changes. The rear tire was much wider (now 240 millimeter), and the fuel tank capacity was expanded to 5 gallons. In 2008, the VRSCAW received the more powerful 1,250-cc version of the Revolution engine and also an optional ABS system for its Brembo brakes. The V-Rod Muscle (VRSCF) is the newest iteration of the V-Rod, introduced in 2009. You can easily spot the Muscle by its unique dual exhausts running down each side of the bike. The VRSCF also has some stylistic changes: Its airbox has large ram intakes (which are purely cosmetic), and the chopped rear fender houses a unique integrated LED brake light and turn signal. The Muscle has the look of a drag bike and the power to back it up.

The liquid-cooled V-Rods are clearly not "traditional" Harleys. Their unique styling and powerful engine set them apart from the rest of the H-D family.

2010 V-Rod Muscle specifications

Drivetrain

Engine:	Revolution
Layout:	60-degree V-twin, rubber-mounted and counterbalanced
Displacement:	76.28 cubic inches (1,250 cc)
Cooling:	Liquid-cooled
Compression ratio:	11.5:1
Fuel system:	Electronic Sequential Port Fuel Injection (ESPFI)
Horsepower:	122 horsepower @ 8,250 rpm
Torque:	86 foot-pounds @ 6,500 rpm
Primary drive:	Chain, 117/64 ratio
Transmission:	Five-speed
Final drive:	Belt

Chassis

Fuel capacity:	5 gallons
Oil capacity:	5 quarts
Wheelbase:	67 inches
Weight:	673 pounds (wet)
Seat height (unlade):	26.7 inches

Suspension

Front:	Telescopic fork, upside-down
Rear:	Twin shocks

Brakes

Front:	2 disc, (four-piston caliper)
Rear:	1 disc (four-piston caliper)
Wheels:	19 inches (front), 18 inches (rear)

What they said

"... [T]he V-Rod delivers more thrills and attention than any other cruiser. And if that's paramount in your buying decision, you owe it to yourself to ride this paradigm-shifting, scene-stealing, knock-your-socks-off new-age Harley."—*Motorcycle USA* (2002 VRSCA V-Rod)

"It's not quite sportbike flickable, but the Street Rod is fun to ride fast in corners. It is definitely the most sporting Harley-Davidson street motorcycle ever."—*Motorcycle Cruiser* (2006 VRSCR Street Rod)

"The wide, angular air-box cover and chopped tail section look as solid and smooth as billet and give the new V-Rod Muscle lines that are clean and powerful."—Paul Crowe, *The Kneeslider* (2009 VRSCF V-Rod Muscle)

"Every time I get to experience the Revolution motor, I'm stunned again by what a fantastic engine it is. The Muscle encourages enthusiastic riding with its great thrust and sweet off-throttle slowing, tactile brakes, slick shifting, and gorgeous styling."—Dave Searle, *Motorcycle Consumer News* (2009 VRSCF V-Rod Muscle)

"The Street Rod reminds me of Honda's last CB–50 Nighthawk, a machine that Honda built because everyone said it should. The Street Rod feels like a motorcycle designed by a committee, a machine that tries to be everything to everyone: cruiser, sportbike, roadster, American Classic. I'd rather have a softail Deuce with the latest stroker kit or a Road King or a Buell XB—all are motorcycles that know exactly what they want to be, each comes for a core of passion, and each is a real American classic." *Cycle World*, April, 2005

Parts prices/cost of typical repairs

Basic service intervals: 1,000 miles, 5,000 miles, every 5,000 miles thereafter.

1,000-mile service: includes all drivetrain fluid changes and 30-point inspection and adjustments, $275 to $350 (at a Harley-Davidson dealer). Total parts costs is typically around $100.

Valve lash service: 15,000-mile intervals. (15,000, 30,000, and so on)

	Labor (hours)	Parts Cost (est.)
Oil and filter	.5	$39.48
Air filter	.3	$48.88
Valve adjustment	3.5	$93.31
Change plugs	.5	$8.60

Source: Motorcycle Consumer News

Recalls and service bulletins

In September 2004, V-Rod motorcycles were recalled for fuel tank concerns. The stock fuel tanks could potentially become over-pressurized and cause fuel to spray out when the fuel cap was removed. The affected bikes were built between June and July 2004. As a safety measure, dealers will test and replace fuel canisters as required.

In July 2007, VRSCR Street Rod models were recalled for an exhaust safety issue. Dealers installed heat shields to protect riders from potential exhaust burns.

Photo by David Blattel

Garage Watch
Key items to look for.

Garage Watch (Key items to look for) Other than high maintenance costs (see previous page) the V-Rod family has proven to be reliable as a (liquid-cooled) stone and has no major trouble areas.

Some riders have reported initial problems with minor coolant and oil leaks.

Some riders have reported unusually high oil consumption during the extended 10,000 mile break-in period.

Photo by David Blattel

In 2003 certain early-model V-Rods were recalled to replace a faulty fuel module flange.

Chapter 25

2008–onward FLST (Softail)

The Softail series is the lynchpin of the Harley lineup, and the Heritage Softail remains one of the most popular members of the Softail family. It's a nostalgic, classic cruiser, wearing leather and fringe and a true open-road bike. It doesn't have the ABS, powerful stereo, or protective fairing of the big touring bikes. Instead, the Heritage Softail is distilled to the essence of an open-road motorcycle—the big V-twin, comfortable saddle, easy handling, and classic styling. The Heritage is iconic Harley.

The Heritage was introduced in 1988 and, in classic H-D fashion, has received incremental improvements over the years. As with all Softails, the Heritage uses the twin shocks and springs that are hidden under the engine. This now-proven layout allows the Heritage to retain its classic styling and provide for a smooth highway ride. The front suspension consists of a large telescopic fork, which still bears a strong resemblance to those of its ancestor, the Panhead-powered Hydra Glide, introduced in 1949.

Despite the classic styling, the powertrain is very contemporary. The Heritage is powered by the solid-mounted 96B, which is counterbalanced to quell vibrations. The fuel-injected powerplant produces 92 foot-pounds of torque, and it is mated to the Cruise Drive six-speed transmission. Thumb the starter and the engine lights right up, whether hot or cold. The counterbalancer does a nice job of smoothing the engine out, and the vibes further diminish as the engine warms up.

Drop the Heritage into gear, and you'll quickly feel at home in the saddle. The Cruise Drive six-speed shifts without the loud clunk of previous transmissions, and the clutch, throttle, and brakes are light to the touch. The seating position is classic long-haul Harley: A deep, soft saddle, an easy reach to the bars, and wide rubber-mounted floorboards for your feet. Work your way through the six gears and the pulse of the 96B is relaxed. At cruising speeds, sixth gear will keep the engine at low revs, which helps fuel economy and reduces vibrations. However, passing on two-lane roads will invariably require a downshift or two.

The highway ride of the Heritage is smooth, and the accommodations make it a natural choice for a touring bike. The leather saddlebags are adorned with the fringes, studs, and conchos that are synonymous with the touring cruiser. The stock seat is well padded and the passenger accommodations are generous for two-up touring. The windshield provides good weather protection and is easily removed without tools for those hot days or slower rides. Of course, there are many accessories for the Heritage, including chrome, luggage, seating, and windshields that allow a rider to personalize the bike to his or her tastes.

Of particular note, the Heritage Softail is a manageable bike for the inseam-challenged rider. The stock seat height is a comfortable 25.5-inches, and the low-speed handling of the Heritage belies its substantial 761-pound curb weight. These factors make it an excellent choice for riders who are uncomfortable with managing a heavier Touring bike. The only modification that might improve the experience could be a shorter set of handlebars. The stock bars on the newest Heritage bikes may be uncomfortably high for some riders.

2010 FLSTC Heritage Softail Classic specifications

Drivetrain

Engine:	Twin Cam 96B
Layout:	45-degree V-twin, counterbalanced
Displacement:	96 cubic inches (1,584 cc)
Cooling:	Air-cooled
Compression ratio:	9.2:1
Fuel system:	Electronic Sequential Port Fuel Injection (ESPFI)
Torque:	92.2 foot-pounds @ 3,000 rpm
Primary drive:	Chain, 34/46 ratio
Transmission:	Six-speed
Final drive:	Belt

Chassis

Fuel capacity:	5.0 gallons
Oil capacity:	3.5 quarts
Wheelbase:	64.5 inches
Weight:	761 pounds (wet)
Seat height (unlade):	25.5 inches

Suspension

Front:	Telescopic fork
Rear:	Twin shocks

Brakes

Front:	1 disc, (four-piston caliper)
Rear:	1 disc (two-piston caliper)
Wheels:	16 inches (front), 16 inches (rear)

What they said

"[T]he Heritage Classic remains first and foremost an old-school bagger, and in that role it excels, proving for the most part as road worthy and distance-friendly as any dedicated touring mount from Milwaukee." —Terry Roorda, *Thunder Press* (2009 Heritage Softail Classic)

"[Y]ou'll be getting a lot for your dollar these days with the Heritage Softail Classic, and that includes both function and style." — Bill Stermer, *American Rider* (2009 Heritage Softail Classic)

"It only takes a look to realize the Heritage Softail Classic is the quintessential American V-Twin cruiser, so there's no need to tamper much with a winning formula."—MotorcycleUSA.com (2009 Heritage Softail Classic)

"While the Harley Davidson Heritage Softail Classic isn't a strict touring motorcycle, the appointments which are given to the Heritage Softail Classic to make it a touring motorcycle more than make up for the lack of a radio or on-board heater." —William Sidney (2008 Heritage Softail Classic)

"When the Harley-Davidson Softail Deluxe was introduced in 2005 many women gravitated to it because it boasted the lowest seat height of any Harley at the time: 24.5 inches. (Since then), it's become one of the more popular motorcycles for women riders. For many women, being able to reach the ground on a big Softail as this is very confidence inspiring."—*Women Riders Now* (2009 Softail Deluxe)

"Any woman wanting to enter the big leagues of motorcycling should consider this motorcycle."—*Women Riders Now* (2009 Softail Deluxe)

"The Harley Davidson Softail Deluxe is a beautiful motorcycle. In many ways, its form and lines are the inspirations of every motorcycle built today, from Japanese cruisers to American Iron."—William Sidney (2009 Softail Deluxe)

"You might not expect such a low-tech-looking motorcycle to work well when the road bends, but the Springer Classic actually provides better cornering clearance than many more modern cruisers and comparable stability when leaned over and dragging."—*Motorcyclist Magazine* (2005 Softail Springer Classic)

"Although relatively small in terms of displacement by comparison to other V-twins, the 1,450-cc Harley engines can more than hold their own in terms of power against most of the 1,500- to 1,700-cc machines."—*Motorcyclist Magazine* (2005 Softail Springer Classic)

"Even my sport-riding buddies grudgingly acknowledged the bike's 'cool' quotient, and the girlfriend was pretty well pleased with the passenger accommodations (can't underestimate the importance of this). Thing is, the Springer's actually a fun bike to ride too."— Andrew Cherney, *Motorcyclist Magazine* (2005 Softail Springer Classic)

Parts prices/cost of typical repairs

1,000-mile service: Includes all drivetrain fluid changes and 30-point inspection and adjustments, $275 to $350 (at a Harley-Davidson dealer). Total parts costs are typically around $100.

Twin Cam 96: Key fluid change intervals.

Engine oil and filter: 1,000-mile service, every 5,000 miles thereafter.

Engine primary chaincase drain: 1,000-mile service, 10,000 miles, then every 10,000 miles thereafter.

Cruise drive transmission drain: 1,000 miles, every 20,000 miles thereafter.

Usability and collectibility ratings

Usability: ★★★★ It's expensive, but the Deluxe is a great motorcycle.

Collectibility: Too early to determine.

Garage Watch
Key items to look for.

Early Twin Cams suffered almost universal catastrophic cam-bearing failures. This problem should have been solved in all bikes still on the road, but make sure.

After the engine was enlarged to 96 cubic inches, engines suffered heating problems. This was mostly solved in later models.

Comfortable saddle and smooth handling.

Stock seat is a comfortable 25.5 inches in height making this a good choice for shorter riders who are uncomfortable with handling a heavier touring bike.

No ABS brakes.

Six-speed transmission shifts without the loud clunk of previous transmissions.

Photo by David Blattel

Engine is counterbalanced to quell vibrations.

For 2004, the Sportster line was reborn. The Motor Company finally blessed the Sporty with a new chassis, which featured a rubber-mounting layout for the engine. With their solid-mounted engines and a lack of counterbalancers, previous Sportsters were notoriously shaky—so much so that cruising speeds of more than 70 miles per hour could only be sustained for short distances before the rider needed to re-establish his or her equilibrium and stand on solid ground.

The new Sportster chassis pulled this bike into the modern age. Sportster owners are no longer required to tighten every fastener on the bike at 100-mile intervals. Important extremities are no longer numb after rides of more than 50 miles. Real-world performance is improved, too, because Sportster riders are now far more likely to rev the engine to its peak rpm without fear of a vibratory assault.

The 883 is the value leader of the Harley lineup. Its price point is the lowest of any Harley (excluding Buells), and its appointments are Spartan when compared to its Big Twin brethren. The base 883 is easily distinguishable by its narrow 3.3-gallon tank. The 883 also features a solo seat, low-rise handlebar, and a mid-set footpeg position. The new chassis also lowered the seat height by about an inch. If the standard 883 is too tall, consider a search for an 883L. Just be warned that the 883L is a "slammed" version of the standard 883. Its rear suspension is significantly stiffer than the standard 883, and its ride quality suffers for it.

The 883 Custom was offered from 2004 to 2009. The Custom has several features that set it apart from other Sportsters and make it a desirable model. The 21-inch wire-spoke wheel gives the Custom some flash, while its narrower, taller tire improves turn-in and handling. The control layout is more relaxed than the standard 883 or 883L. The handlebars are closer to the rider and the footpegs are forward-mounted, befitting the "Custom" moniker. The Custom has a larger fuel tank—4.5 gallons—that significantly changes the overall style of the bike, and its added capacity offers a welcome gain in fuel range too.

As the Sportster line has evolved since 2004, Harley has tweaked its model offerings to match new market trends. For 2010, the 883 Sportsters are only offered in 2 versions—the 883L and the Iron 883. The Iron 883 is a blacked-out version of the standard 883. The engine cases and 13-spoke wheels are finished in a black powdercoat, and the tank and fenders are painted with matte Black Denim and Silver Denim. The black drag-style handlebars, chopped rear fender, and side-mounted license plate give the Iron a tough custom look, though these features come at a price premium of $1,000 more than the 883L.

The Sportster 883 is frequently portrayed as the entry-level Harley—a new Harley owner's first step toward the goal of a Big Twin. Recent Harley-Davidson sales incentive programs reinforce this notion, guaranteeing the trade-in value of a Sportster if it is traded for a Big Twin bike within a year. But that belittles the capability of the 883. The new chassis and its vastly improved vibration isolation have transformed the Sportster into a true daily-driver and a bike worthy of consideration for long-term ownership.

2010 Iron 883 specifications

Drivetrain

Engine:	Evolution
Layout:	45-degree V-twin, rubber-mounted
Displacement:	53.9 cubic inches (883 cc)
Cooling:	Air-cooled
Compression ratio:	8.9:1
Fuel system:	Electronic Sequential Port Fuel Injection (ESPFI)
Torque:	55 foot-pounds @ 3,500 rpm
Primary drive:	Chain, 57/34 ratio
Transmission:	5-speed
Final drive:	Belt

Chassis

Fuel capacity:	3.3 gallons
Oil capacity:	2.8 quarts
Wheelbase:	60 inches
Weight:	565 pounds (wet)
Seat height (unlade):	25.3 inches

Suspension

Front:	Telescopic fork
Rear:	Twin shocks

Brakes

Front:	1 disc, (two-piston caliper)
Rear:	1 disc (one-piston caliper)
Wheels:	19 inches (front), 16 inches (rear)

What they said

"All aspects of the 2004 Harley Sportsters are influenced or overshadowed by the fact that the motorcycle no longer rattles your teeth when you ride it. The motorcycles in the series manage to look every inch Sportsters, but you no longer have to steel yourself for a shaking up when you climb on."—Art Friedman, *Motorcycle Cruiser* (2004 Sportster 883)

"Even at my modest five-foot-eight height the position of the footpegs caused my knees to ride oddly high. The Iron's reduced-travel rear shocks and thin seat are best suited for short riders."—Kevin Duke, Motorcycle.com (2010 Iron 883)

"Harley struck the perfect balance between blackened bits and chrome tips on the Iron 883. Dark enough to run with the sinister sister Dynas and Softails in the DC line, yet still a machine with its own character."—Alfonse Palaima, Motorcycle.com (2010 Iron 883)

"Shorter folks and novices will appreciate the confident footing achieved at stops when settled into the comfortable, dished solo saddle. The mid-mount foot controls and low-rise drag bar provide a natural riding posture and deliver an excellent sense of command."—*Cycle World* (2009 Iron 883)

Parts prices/cost of typical repairs

Air filter: Check every 2,500 miles; replace every 5,000 miles.

1,000-mile service: Includes all drivetrain fluid changes and 30-point inspection and adjustments, $275 to $350 (at a Harley-Davidson dealer). Total parts cost is typically $100.

Sportster Evolution: Key fluid change intervals.

Engine oil and filter: 1,000-mile service, 5,000-mile service, every 5,000 miles thereafter.

Transmission lubricant: 1,000-mile service, 5,000-mile service, every 5,000 miles thereafter.

The new transmission case eliminated the "trap door" that allowed access to the transmission in prior models. The cases must now be split to access transmission internals.

Usability and collectibility ratings

Usability: ★★★★ The 2004 redesign turned the Sportster into a functional motorcycle.

Collectibility: It's too early to assess the collectability of this model.

Recalls and service bulletins

In January 2007, model year 2007 XL883s were recalled to relocate the voltage regulator. The voltage regulator on bikes manufactured between May and November 2006 can contact the front fender under certain conditions, and a new mounting bracket should be installed to prevent obstruction of steering control.

Garage Watch
Key items to look for.

Some riders would like to have a cushier seat than what the stock unit provides.

Model year 2007 XL883s were recalled to install a heat shield on the exhaust as a safety feature.

The new frame on the 2004s is much stouter than that found in previous models and features rubber mounts that reduce engine vibration problems considerably.

Sportsters have always had clunky shifting, especially from neutral to first. Most riders simply learn to live with it.

Chapter 27

2004–onward Sportster 1200

For 2004, Sportsters were completely re-engineered. The Sportster retained its traditional styling, but the overhaul included a new engine and a new frame. The new frame is far stouter than the previous one, and it incorporates rubber mounts to reduce the engine's vibrations. The new engine is almost exactly the same engine that Erik Buell installed in the Buell XBs. Buell improved the 1200 by using lighter pistons and con rods, a revised oiling system with piston oiling jets and expanded oil capacity, plus ported heads and new camshafts.

The latest generation of the Sportster has evolved into several model variations. Ranging from cruiser to sport-oriented, the 1200 model range offers a little of something for every taste. The XL1200C is the chromed-out Custom, which is covered in chrome and brightwork. It features a 21-inch spoke front wheel and lavish chrome from headlight to taillight. The cosmetics also include a two-tone paint scheme on the 4.5-gallon fuel tank. The new chassis allowed for a slimmer oil tank to be located under the seat, making the bike narrower and easier for riders with short-inseams to reach their feet to the ground.

The antithesis of the XL1200C is the Nightster. The XL1200N Nightster was added to the Sportster range for 2008, and it was an immediate hit. The modern-retro Nightster takes its styling cues from the classic bobbers—shortened front and rear fenders, a custom taillight and side-mount license setup, and an ultra-low 26.3-inch seat height enhance the bike's bobber style. As a part of the Harley "Dark Custom" group, the Nightster lives up to its name with blacked-out fenders, rims, hubs, triple clamps, and fork. The engine cases are finished in a medium gray, with both black and polished accents, and the 3.3-gallon fuel tank receives a matte silver or black finish.

The Nightster is undeniably stylish, looking every bit the badass bobber that it intends to be. But this custom look comes at a price—ride comfort. The short rear suspension travel and hard solo seat make the Nightster a short-trip bike that is better suited to bar-hopping than eating up the highway miles. The mitigating factors are the mid-mounted foot controls that allow riders to use their legs to cushion against big bumps in the road.

Taking the bobber look one step further is the Sportster Forty Eight. The Forty Eight debuted late in the 2010 model year, and it shares many of the styling touches of the Nightster—solo seat, bobbed fenders, and a blacked-out engine. Setting it apart are its tiny 2.1-gallon "peanut" fuel tank and forward controls.

The XR1200 is a major departure from the cruiser and custom-styled 1200 Sportsters. This performance-oriented Sportster draws heavily on styling cues from the XR750 dirt tracker, and it brings some additional horsepower to the party too. The XR1200 is powered by a mildly retuned version of the Buell XB engine. It produces a claimed 90-horsepower at 7,000 rpm and 73.8 pound-feet of torque at 3,700 rpm. The XR1200 is also blessed with triple disc brakes and a performance-tuned suspension, making it easily the best-performing Sportster in the lineup.

2010 Nightster specifications

Drivetrain

Engine:	Evolution
Layout:	45-degree V-twin, rubber-mounted
Displacement:	73.4 cubic inches (1,200 cc)
Cooling:	Air-cooled
Compression ratio:	9.7:1
Fuel system:	Electronic Sequential Port Fuel Injection (ESPFI)
Torque:	79 pound-feet @ 4,000 rpm
Primary drive:	Chain, 57/38 ratio
Transmission:	Five-speed
Final drive:	Belt

Chassis

Fuel capacity:	3.3 gallon
Oil capacity:	2.8 quarts
Wheelbase:	60 inch
Weight:	562 pounds (wet)
Seat height (unlade):	26.3 inch

Suspension

Front:	Telescopic fork
Rear:	Twin shocks

Brakes

Front:	1 disc, (2-piston caliper)
Rear:	1 disc (1-piston caliper)
Wheels:	19 inches (front), 16 inches (rear)

What they said

"I wanted the bike to look illegal."—Rich Christoph, Nightster designer, quoted in *Cycle World* (2007 Nightster)

"What impresses me about the Nightster is that we finally have a Sportster that's low enough and agile enough for confident beginners, yet has tons of attitude, style and power, qualities often sacrificed in an entry level motorcycle. And that's a reason to hold on to the Nightster long after you feel you've outgrown it."—Genevieve Schmitt, Women Riders Now.com (2008 Nightster)

"The XR1200 is a fun bike to ride on twisty roads, and in the hands of a fast rider will give a good account of itself in the company of other sportbikes. And we can't imagine saying that about any previous Sportster."—Danny Coe, *Motorcycle Consumer News* (2009 XR1200)

"No matter where we rode the bike, it performed even better than advertised. The motor delivered far more power and torque than we were used to from any of the earlier Sportsters. The new stiffer frame design coupled with the rubber-mounted engine provided a very different experience than we had ever had on a Sportster. We could actually feel the interaction between the tires and the asphalt, whereas in the past, engine vibrations masked this."—*Hot Bike* (2004 XL1200C Sportster)

Parts prices/cost of typical repairs

Air filter: Check every 2,500 miles; replace every 5,000 miles.

1,000-mile service: Includes all drivetrain fluid changes and 30-point inspection and adjustments: $275 to $350 (at a Harley-Davidson dealer). Total parts cost is typically around $100.

Sportster Evolution: Key fluid change intervals.

Engine oil and filter: 1,000-mile service, 5,000-mile service, every 5,000 miles thereafter.

Transmission lubricant: 1,000-mile service, 5,000-mile service, every 5,000 miles thereafter.

Usability and collectibility ratings

Usability: ★★★★★ The 1200 version of the Sportster is even more practical than the 883 version, thanks to more power.

Collectibility: It's too early to assess the collectability of this model.

Garage Watch
Key items to look for.

After the 2004 redesign, the Sportster in both 883 and 1200 form has proven remarkably reliable and trouble free.

Some riders would like to have a cushier seat than what the stock unit provides.

Sportsters have always had clunky shifting, especially from neutral to first. Most riders simply learn to live with it.

Model year 2007 1200s were recalled to install a heat shield on the exhaust as a safety feature.

Photo by David Blattel

The new frame on the 2004 model is much stouter than that found in previous models and features rubber mounts that reduce engine vibration problems considerably.

Harley-Davidson's customer base has aged over the years, and the company has turned toward the touring models to fill demand. More comfortable and luxurious than other Harleys, the touring bikes retain Harley's classic styling yet integrate some of the industry's latest technologies. Their popularity has inspired a host of technological improvements and new model variants.

Touring bikes for 2008 received major changes. Brembo brakes were now standard equipment, and ABS control was available on all Touring models as an extra-cost option. Power for these models comes from the rubber-mounted Twin Cam 96 engine. This 1,584-cc engine is standard equipment in FLs (with the exception of the trikes and 110-cubic-inch CVO models), and it is mated to the six-speed Cruise Drive transmission.

For 2009, Harley-Davidson underpinned its Touring models with a completely new chassis and swingarm. Built with forged castings and boxed sheet metal, the new chassis is stout from the steering head to the swingarm. The chassis retains the classic dimensions and look of the older models, but it resists the twisting and flexing that plagued those models.

To say that the performance of this new chassis was an improvement over the prior models would be a major understatement. To quote Motorcycle.com, "We are convinced it was one of the best things the Motor Company has ever done for its products." Steering response and the suspension's ride control were drastically improved. The "wallowing" tendencies were gone, and riders were treated to a smoother, much more controlled ride. A fringe benefit is that the model year 2009 Touring bikes are rated to carry an extra 70 pounds of passengers and gear, compared to the 2008 models.

New variants of the FL continue to appear. The popularity of the Street Glide (introduced for model year 2006) inspired the Road Glide Custom, which shares its lowered rear stance and simple, clean style. The Road Glide Custom replaced the standard Road Glide completely for model year 2010. The Electra Glide Ultra Limited also bowed in 2010. This top-of-the-line Ultra features an air-adjustable suspension, electronic cruise control, heated grips, and premium luggage compartment. The Ultra Limited is powered by the Twin Cam 103 engine, mated to the Cruise Drive transmission.

The FLHTCUTG Tri Glide Ultra Classic appeared as a new model for model year 2009. This trike was designed cooperatively with Lehman Trikes. When introduced, it was offered at an MSRP of $29,999—substantially less than the cost of a trike "conversion" from a two-wheeled Electra Glide. The Tri-Glide Ultra Classic is powered by the Twin Cam 103, and its features include ABS, air-adjustable suspension, and electronic cruise control. The trike lineup expanded for model year 2010 with the introduction of the Street Glide Trike (FLHXX). Fewer amenities are standard on the Street Glide Trike, but ABS and cruise control are optional.

Harley offered several CVO Touring models for model year 2010. The CVO Ultra Classic and CVO Street Glide feature special wheels as well as chrome and paint upgrades that are common to all CVO models. They are powered by the Twin Cam 110 engines, mated to the six-speed Cruise Drive transmission.

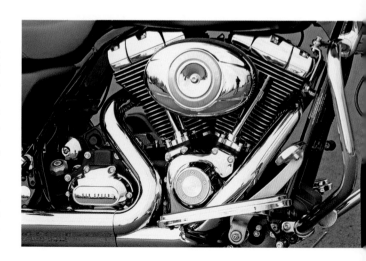

2009 FLHR Road King Specifications

Drivetrain

Engine:	Twin cam 96
Layout:	45-degree V-twin
Displacement:	96 cubic inches (1,584 cc)
Cooling:	Air-cooled
Compression ratio:	9.2:1
Fuel system:	Electronic Sequential Port Fuel Injection (ESPFI)
Torque:	92.6 foot-pounds @ 3,500 rpm
Primary drive:	Chain, 34/46 ratio
Transmission:	Six-speed
Final drive:	Belt

Chassis

Fuel capacity:	6 gallons
Oil capacity:	4 quarts
Wheelbase:	63.5 inches
Weight:	812 pounds (wet)
Seat height (unlade):	29.9 inches

Suspension

Front:	Telescopic fork
Rear:	Twin shocks

Brakes

Front:	2 disc, (four-piston caliper)
Rear:	1 disc (four-piston caliper)
Wheels:	17 inches (front), 16 inches (rear)

What they said

"Fit and finish is superb, and easy controls and light steering are unexpected surprises."— *Motorcycle Cruiser* (2010 Electra Glide Ultra Limited)

"Wonderfully absent . . . is the eye-popping hinge-in-the-middle-of-the-frame sensation."—Motorcycle.com (Commenting on the new Touring frame, 2009 Electra Glide Ultra Classic)

"H-D's touring motorcycles are not only the most comfortable to ride, but also are the most fun—especially on curvy pavement." —Motorcycle-usa.com

"By beefing up their chassis and running gear, Harley-Davidson has brought the FL Touring bikes' handling into the 21st century, without sacrificing the 20th-century style and tradition that makes motorcycles like the Ultra so popular with touring riders."—*Rider* (2009 Electra Glide Ultra Classic)

Parts prices/cost of typical repairs

1,000-mile service: Includes drivetrain fluid changes and 30-point inspection and adjustments, $275 to $350 (at a Harley-Davidson dealer). Total parts costs are typically around $100.

Usability and collectibility ratings

Usability: ★★★★★ A new frame made these touring bikes the equal of any in the world.

Collectibility: It's too early to assess the status of this model in the collectors market.

Recalls and service bulletins

In December 2009, 111,000 Harley Touring bikes were recalled to repair the front fuel tank mounts. In the event of a crash, the mounts may distort and cause the tank to leak. Virtually all 2009–2010 Touring bikes are affected, making this one of the largest recalls in Harley history.

Garage Watch
Key items to look for.

After the 2004 redesign, the Sportster in both 883 and 1200 form has proven remarkably reliable and trouble free.

Some models had problems with rubber mounts on the rear fenders and exhaust falling off. It's a cheap and easy fix.

2009 Harley touring bikes are rated to carry an extra 70 lbs. of passengers and gear, compared to the 2008 models.

A defect in the neutral safety switch on the 2007 model should have been fixed.

Chassis significantly improved beginning with 2004 models.

Photo by David Blattel

Chapter 29

2007–onward FXD (Dyna)4-1

In recent years, the Dyna family has occupied the position of the least-costly Big Twins in the Harley lineup. Their styling retains the classic look of the stripped-down customs of the 1970s, but their performance and handling have received steady updates over the years.

The Dyna family received a major chassis redesign in model year 2006 receiving a new, stiffer chassis. More important, the Twin Cam 96 engine was introduced into the Dynas in model year 2007. The rubber-mounted Twin Cam 96 engine develops significantly more power than the Twin Cam 88, and it is mated to the familiar Cruise Drive six-speed transmission. Other shared features are the under-seat battery box and exposed twin rear shocks.

A new Dyna model arrived in 2008, the FXDF Dyna Fat Bob. The Fat Bob joined the rest of the Dyna family: Street Bob, Low Rider, and Super Glide custom. The Fat Bob blended in well with the existing Dyna family and incorporated some unique styling touches, such as its twin round headlamps, 16-inch cast-aluminum wheels and wide front tire (130 millimeters), 2-into-1-into-2 exhaust, and a bulbous 5.1-gallon fuel tank. Despite its intimidating look, flat drag bars, and forward foot controls, the Fat Bob is comfortable and nimble. It's stable on the highway and the rubber-mounted Twin Cam 96 is smooth and has plenty of power. The Fat Bob was offered in seven colors, including three matte-finish "denim" colors.

After taking a hiatus from the lineup for 2007, the Dyna Wide Glide returned as a 2008 model. For 2008, the FXDWG Wide Glide was offered as a limited-edition model, wearing limited-edition 105th Anniversary touches that included two-tone Copper Pearl and Vivid Black paint and special tank badging. With its raked front end (34 degrees!), low seat, internal handlebar wiring, and 21-inch spoke front wheel, the Wide Glide is the epitome of what a factory custom should be.

The Wide Glide was again mothballed for the 2009 model year, before returning to full production status as a 2010 model. The 2010 Wide Glide is lower, cleaner, and darker, a nod to the popularity of dark customs. The engine and cases are now blacked-out with sparse chrome and polished surfaces, and the wheels get black powder coating too. The already-slammed suspension of the Wide Glide retains its namesake wide-spaced fork but is now even lower at both ends, and this puts the seat height at just 25.5 inches off the pavement. The rear fender is shortened, and the rear lighting consists of twin red-lens turn-signal lamps that illuminate simultaneously under braking.

Despite their raked-out custom appearance, the Dynas are comfortable and easy to ride. The style is undeniably cool, and the late models' low seat heights make them accessible to a wider range of riders. The seats are firm and supportive, the handlebar reach is reasonable (in stock form), and the road manners are accomplished. Cornering clearance is good for a long-wheelbase cruiser, though the exhaust on the right side of the bike can be quick to grind the pavement under hard cornering.

2010 FXDWG Dyna Wide Glide specifications

Drivetrain

Engine:	Twin Cam 96
Layout:	45-degree V-twin
Displacement:	96 cubic inches (1,584 cc)
Cooling:	Air-cooled
Compression ratio:	9.2:1
Fuel system:	Electronic Sequential Port Fuel Injection (ESPFI)
Torque:	92.0 foot-pounds @ 3,000 rpm
Primary drive:	Chain, 34/46 ratio
Transmission:	Six-speed
Final drive:	Belt

Chassis

Fuel capacity:	4.7 gallons
Oil capacity:	3 quarts
Wheelbase:	68.3 inches
Weight:	665 pounds (wet)
Seat height (unlade):	25.5 inches

Suspension

Front:	Telescopic fork
Rear:	Twin shocks

Brakes

Front:	1 disc, (four-piston caliper)
Rear:	1 disc (two-piston caliper)
Wheels:	21 inches (front), 17 inches (rear)

What they said

"The first thing you'll probably notice on a Fat Bob is that you sit in the bike, not on it. A roomy, comfortable seat cradles you behind the large tank."—Basem Wasef, About.com (2008 Dyna Fat Bob)

"At cruising speeds, the motor is very smooth, but at idle and low revs, vibration is quite prevalent. As with all modern Harley powerplants, throttle response is excellent, reacting smoothly and precisely."—Motorcycle.com (2010 Dyna Wide Glide)

"All-in-all, the Dyna Fat Bob has unique, aggressive styling and performs surprisingly well through the corners. The rubber-mounted twin cam 96 engine is very smooth, and pulls with authority."—*Motorcycle Daily* (2008 Dyna Fat Bob)

"The Dyna Wide Glide is a downright fun motorcycle to own. Both women and men will appreciate the friendly ergonomics and the easy handling. It's not recommended for beginners, but certainly after a few years of riding, the Wide Glide makes a nice move up from a Sportster or other smaller displacement motorcycle."—Genevieve Schmitt, *Women Riders Now* (2010 Dyna Wide Glide)

Garage Watch
Key items to look for.

Early Twin Cams suffered almost universal catastrophic cam-bearing failures. This problem should have been solved in all bikes still on the road, but make sure.

After the engine was enlarged to 96 cubic inches, engines suffered heating problems. This was mostly solved in later models.

The 2010 model Wide Glide got even lower and now has a seat height of 25.5- inches which is great news for shorter riders.

The exhaust on the ride side of the bike can be quick grind the pavement under hard cornering.

On 2007 FXDWG models check the hole in the handlbars where the wires exit between the handlebar clamps for cracks. A recall at that time saw many of these handlebars replaced.

The Twin-Cam engine introduced in the 2007 model provides significantly more power than the Twin-Cam 88 found in previous year models.

Photo by David Blattel

Parts prices/cost of typical repairs

1,000-mile service: Includes all drivetrain fluid changes and 30-point inspection and adjustments, $275 to $350 (at Harley-Davidson dealer). Total parts costs is typically around $100.
Twin Cam 96: Key fluid change intervals
Engine oil and filter: 1,000-mile service, every 5,000 miles thereafter.
Engine primary chaincase drain: 1,000-mile service, 10,000-mile service, every 10,000 miles thereafter.
Cruise drive transmission drain: 1,000 miles, every 20,000 miles thereafter.

Usability and collectibility ratings

Usability: ★★★★ The Dyna frame was a revelation when introduced in 1991. Today it is getting a bit long in tooth.

Collectibility: It's too early to assess the status of this model in the collectors market.

Photo by David Blattel